# The Finn Chronicles:
# Year Two

## A dog's reports from the front lines of hooman rescue

*by Finnegan Count Smooshie Tushie*
*as transcribed by Gwen Romack*

Published by Off Leash Press

Julie loves me so much she turned me into fine art!
#IThinkImEvenMoreHandsomeInGraphite

Artist: Julie Goldman
Medium: Graphite on Strathmore 500 Series Bristol Board

I dedicate this book to frozen dairy slop and bacon (yes, again, because it matters that much).
It's also dedicated to all the essential workers out there risking their lives to keep our society running during a global pandemic. Healthcare workers, grocery workers, truckers, post office employees, growers, and the rest.
Thank you for helping us stay safe.
We hope this book brings you some much needed laughter and light during these difficult times.

# Contents

# Introduction

"DOGS ARE NOT OUR WHOLE LIFE, BUT THEY MAKE OUR LIVES WHOLE."

– Rodger A. Caras

My name is Finnegan Count Smooshie Tushie, but I go by Finn for short. I'm a mix of the regal and intense Hungarian Vizsla, the vocal and intense Beagle, and the sensitive and stubborn Pittie. Basically, a perfect combination of intensity, volume and intensity!

As a top graduate of the K9 Rescue Academy, I was given some really challenging hoomans for my rescue assignment. I write reports back to rescue headquarters that they use to help train the younger cadets and update our files about the hoomans and their strange rituals. It's been a challenge training these hoomans, but I've come to love them. I've got a hairy hooman I call Daddy and a squishy hooman I call Mommy.

This book includes my second year of reports and adventures. You should go back and read the first one if you haven't already. We lay the groundwork for critical philosophical and mathematical theorems in that book that you need to understand before proceeding to this one. Just

kidding. But it does help you get to know me and my hoomans.

I've got The Squishy One doing the social media for me and a YouTube channel where you can find videos that go along with some of my finnanigans in this book! There's also loads of bonus content for endless fun and cuteness.

Finnstagram: @finnchronicles
Finnbook:
https://www.facebook.com/FinnChronicles
My website:
https://www.thefinnchronicles.com
YouTube:
https://www.youtube.com/c/FinnTheDog
(Check out the *Year Two Playlist* for videos from my second year that you'll recognize from the stories. These are linked throughout in the ebook version, but you can find them all at the YouTube link above as well.)

# Week Fifty-Four

March 23, 2019 ·

HI, EVERYONE. FINN HERE with my week 54 report. It's been a pretty good week at Chateau Finn, except for all the rain. I focused a lot of energy this week on The Hairy One. After our big fight (when they came back from abandoning me), I thought our relationship needed some extra attention. #YoullLoseItIfYouSnoozeIt

I still haven't figured out the strange ritual of the hoomans pee peeing and poo pooing inside the room with the terrible no good bathtub on a white throne that steals their stinky stuff. Apparently, the thief throne was broken, and Daddy had to fix it. I tried to supervise him, but he kept locking me out of the room. This made my supervisory efforts much harder. I had to cry and bark my constructive criticism through the glass door. #GrassIsNeverBroken #JustSayin

He eventually emerged and we went on an epic bro-walk at the park. We took selfies and even ran around the play area together chasing birds. We also saw the biggest dogs I've ever seen ever. Daddy called them "horses" and said we couldn't play with them. But I really, really wanted to. He took me near enough to smell them and flash them an award-winning smile. I like his strategy. We'll charm them with a slow build-up to our relationship and then once we're old pals, we will jump on them to initiate play. #SolidPlanPops

That night we were all tired, so we had some Netflix and chill time in the big bed. I don't understand why we can't just watch Animal Planet all the time, but they won't do it. #INeedToKnowIfTheGazelleGotAway

I also worked on The Hairy One's playtime obedience through active wrestling sessions this week. We had several good rounds of play that help me to establish I'm the boss while showing him I care by chewing on him like a prized antler. I chew on him, he yells, "no bites!!" and I bite more. It's our thing. He pretends he means it, but what he really means is "more bites!!" The wrestling also helps me keep my skills sharp in case I ever come face to face with an alligator or puma. #ISawItOnAnimalPlanet

Daddy and I also had some grooming and cuddle time in mommy's office which she kept rudely interrupting. I tried to make clear that she better back off. #HesMine

The most exciting part of the week was a special gotchaversary gift from Kathy!!! She sent me a smelly-good box of bones that's bigger than me!!!! They are delicious. I was a very good boy when presented with the open box. It was hard to be so restrained, but I did it. And I've gotten a bone every day since as my reward!!! #ThankYouKathy #BonesAreMyFavoriteHowdYouKnow

That's all the news and #Finnanigans from this week. Over and out.

# Week Fifty-Five

March 30, 2019 ·

HI, EVERYONE. FINN HERE with my week 55 report. It's been a long 55 weeks since being assigned these hoomans to rescue. I'm pleased to report their training is sticking more and more each week, and they're finally understanding I'm in charge. This week was a particularly good one with the hoomans, but somewhat difficult regarding my occupational health and safety duties. #ComplianceMatters

On Sunday, the hoomans surprised me with a Viz Whizz pawty!! I got to see all my Vizsla friends again for Sedona's 1st birthday! We played so hard, chased each other and even got a delicious treat the hoomans called a "pupaccino." The Hairy One gave me one, and man, was it amazing. So I sidled up to some nice ladies at the pawty and gave my best pitiful face until I scored a second one! #PuppyDogEyesForTheWin

The Hairy One spent most of the pawty chasing me down, making me stop kissing or humping, and apologizing to the other hoomans. They kept calling me things like "Casanova" and "Kissy Bandit," I remain unclear why he kept pulling me off my lady friends. It was just when things were getting good. #PawtyPooper The Squishy One says now I'm probably on some kind of list at Viz Whizz HQ for being "overly

affectionate." Whatever that means.
#TheresNoSuchThingAsOverlyAffectionate

The Hairy One and I decided to exclude The Squishy One from daily staff meetings for one week – to teach her a lesson about always dominating the agenda. But the plan backfired once we realized we had no agenda without her. After a few minutes of mindless brainstorming about our activity and meal plans for the day (which we didn't know because Mommy makes those for us), we realized this strategy wasn't going to fly. I decided to use our remaining time chewing on Daddy's face and mean-mugging the camera.
#HeInsistedOnSelfies

Spring has sprung here at Chateau Finn, and that means I got two back-to-back outside days at camp this week!! The outside area is my favorite, and it's much bigger than inside. I can really get up to maximum velocity out there and come home much more tired than indoor days. This means focused snuggle time on The Squishy One under a blanket when I get home.
#ThatsWhenHerSquishinessComesInHandy

On outside days, I like to get the whole pack lathered up into what I call a "dognado" and then reward each one with a kiss.
#ThatsWhyTheyCallMeTheKissyBandit

Spring has also brought some new health and safety issues that I'm working to address. Our primary homestead is in a very rural area with a lot of nature all around us. It's bad enough I have to monitor year-round for hawks, robins, crows and vultures. But all the sudden I've got skunks, bunnies, groundhogs and fox to manage as well. Not to mention the airplanes! Those terrify me, but only during my nighttime potty breaks. #TheyAreTheBiggestBirdsEver

My attempts at nature-management are usually met with irritating obstacles and lectures from the hoomans. I grow weary of their interference. Yes, I know that's a groundhog and they have razor nails. No, I don't want my nose chopped off. But did they ever consider that maybe I would kick that groundhog's butt?!? Noooooo! They won't even give me a chance to show what I've got. #TheyDontBelieveInMe The Squishy One even feeds the bunnies and birds!?! What is wrong with her? I've tried to tell her to stop that, but she won't listen. She claims the bunnies are not a danger and I'm not allowed to hurt them. #ShesNotTheBrightestBulb

A skunk appears to have taken up residence under our front porch and we engage in a silent-but-smelly battle each night when I go out for my last patrol. So far, she hasn't managed to get me, but her warning shots linger for hours - coming in through the cracked windows in our room upstairs. I like to terrify her as soon as my paws hit the porch decking and wake up the whole town with my fierceness. #OneDayVictoryWillBeMine

That's all the news and #Finnanigans from this week. Over and out.

# Special Report

April 3, 2019 ·

Everyone has that one coworker that just never carries their weight. #Slacker #HowIsThisComfortable

# Week Fifty-Six
April 6, 2019 ·

HI, EVERYONE. FINN HERE with my week 56 report. My hoomans have been a real delight this week. The Hairy One has been extra attentive and The Squishy One has been extra loose with the treats. I even got to have outside camp two days in a row!! And to top it off, they surprised me with a trip to the alternate dwelling. I just love it here. #LifeIsGood #ItsGoodToBeMe

The Squishy One wasn't feeling great on Tuesday so we worked from bed part of the day. It's a lot harder to micromanage her from bed and she's constantly hogging the laptop. I did my best to snoopervise, though. #SheForgotTheCoverMemoOnTheTPSReport

Upon arrival at the alternate dwelling late Thursday night, I performed the customary security check. Finding no threats, I dove into my toy basket to find my big blue squeaky bone. I love getting here and inspecting my toys and blankies to make sure no one else has touched them while we were gone. #MyPreciouses

Friday's staff meeting was intense. The Hairy One and I had a breakout discussion about the "treat to good boy" ratio that got heated. Some things were said that we both regret. We called in HR and she helped us agree to disagree. Then we made up with a no-girls-allowed snuggle-fest. #ConstructiveConflictTrainingWorks

I've also resumed my alternate-dwelling neighborhood watch duties. I monitor things from the front door and alert when I see any kind of bird or critter. I also bark my face off during our early morning walks to let all the neighbors know we're in town. Neither is particularly appreciated by the hoomans, though. They tell me to be quiet and I wonder how they made it this far in life without my protection. #NotTheBrightestBulbs

I'm hoping to score a walk on the beach tomorrow morning and maybe turbo-dig some sand holes. #TheTinyCrabsTerrifyMeAndItsExhilarating

That's all the news and #Finnanigans from this week. Over and out.

# Special Report

April 10, 2019 ·

Hiiiiiii Mama. Whatcha got there?

# Week Fifty-Seven

April 13, 2019 ·

HI, EVERYONE. FINN HERE with my week 57 report. This report is coming to you from a soggy doggy that got caught in the rain during my Saturday morning patrol.
#IDoNotLikePinaColadas
#WetAndMadAboutIt

Monday started off with a surprise date with my #1 girlfriend, Jessica. She missed me over the winter and was so happy to see me again.
#LLFinn #ReunitedAndItFeelsSoGood

Our staff meetings were mostly a snooze fest this week until I accidentally referred to The Hairy One by name in front of HR and got a twenty-minute lecture on "respect at work" again. Listen, I can't help that he's hairy, OK? It's hair, but in all the places fur should be. I guess accuracy is not one of our corporate values.
#WaitUntilHRHearsWhatICallTheOtherOne

The hoomans took me to the boardwalk where, upon realizing we were near the gigantic bathtub, I dramatically threw myself down flat as a pancake to prevent any forward motion. I know at this point the "dramatically" part is just assumed, right? After some coaxing, I remembered the smells, people, other dogs and even the gigantic bathtub can be fun and I got on board. #SeeWhatIDidThere #GotOnBoard

I'd like to put in a request for HQ researchers to do some benchmarking with the other agents. How can I get fun romps in the gigantic fun bathtub without getting put in the horrible home bathtub when we

get back? Who has solved this problem with their hoomans? #BathsMakeMeWetAndSmelly

One of the lower points in the week was a major backslide with the hoomans' training. They had been doing pretty well with meeting my constant and particular needs until this week. This week they reverted back to shoving my treats into an evil rubber toy and expecting ME to work for them. Me!? #IHavePeopleForThat

I've enclosed a number of videos showing my attempts to coach them about their bad choices. I begged and pleaded for help but The Squishy One just laughed at me and took video! I finally decided to at least try to get the treats out myself and after a few minutes it was empty. Then I protested the emptiness. The Squishy One kept calling me a "diva" and "Mariah Carey" and laughing. #Madness #ICantLiveLikeThis #WhoIsMariahCarey

The Akita up the street is still messing with me. He strolled by this week and mean-mugged me. The hoomans caught it on video with the perfect song playing. #TurnOnSound #TroubleTroubleTrouble

That's all the news and #Finnanigans from this week. Over and out.

# Week Fifty-Eight

April 20, 2019 ·

HI, EVERYONE. FINN HERE with my week 58 report. Listen, I know the life of a rescuer dog isn't glamorous. I knew when I signed up that part of my duties would include Brene Brown and Oprah Netflix specials and long boring conversations about esoteric hooman things. But lately, geez. The Squishy One has been on a roll about changing our diets, our attitudes and our perspectives on life. I try to explain to her the only change The Hairy One and I want to see is #MoreBacon but she is relentless. #AskMeAboutLoveLanguages #Snooze

The big upside to her new kick is extra-long walks on the boardwalk and in the sand by the huge bathtub. There are so many birds and sooo much food spilled on the ground to sniff (ok, and sometimes lick if I'm quick enough). Hoomans drop a lot of ice cream on the boardwalk and just leave it there! #Wasteful #Lunatics

The downside is pictures. She keeps stopping us for pictures. I generally refuse to look at the camera which only extends the torture. But I do love hearing her voice change to fake happy, fake happier, fake excited, and then annoyed as she begs me to look at her for a shot. #NuhUhWontDoIt #WhatsThatCantHearYaSquishy

I'm not one to complain (unless I have to... which is daily), but I get horrible service around here. The hoomans insist on waking up at different times on different days. They eat at random times. They even poop at random times! It's like I'm living in an asylum of spontaneous lunatics. Meeting my needs should be their #1 priority and it just never is. Just the other day, I had to get ugly to secure my post-breakfast treat they call a "there's nothing in there bud it's just a pill pocket." It's supposed to be delivered directly to my treat-hole precisely one second after my last swallow of food. But no. The Hairy One just wandered around the kitchen like an idiot doing Dog knows what. I hated having to do it, but I staged quite the protest to get his attention and remedy this atrocity. #MyLoveLanguageIsRoutine

Morning staff meetings were mostly uneventful this week. I chose Mommy for 1x1s to make Daddy jealous and get him back on his A game. And my allergies were rough this week, so cuddles with The Squishy One were in order. #IMakeHerWipeOffMyEyeBoogies

FEELING CUTE.... MIGHT THROW A TANTRUM LATER... IDK

I also got a mani/pedi at the vet this week. They love me there, so it really made their day to get a visit. However, some hoomans there willfully ignore me and it's just not ok. They just walk by and do other things without loving on me!!! It's outrageous. I voiced my displeasure throughout the proceedings with some choice protest tantrums. Ok, I stayed laying down for one of them - not my best work. But they still picked up what I was putting down. #IRequireConstantAttention #IdLikeToLickYouHoomanComeHere

That's all the news and #Finnanigans from this week. Over and out.

# Week Fifty-Nine

April 27, 2019 ·

HI, EVERYONE. FINN HERE with my week 59 report. I demand a raise. The hoomans took me on a strange and long adventure that ended at yet another alternative dwelling in a place called "Williamsburg." This dwelling was enormous. Hundreds of rooms and so many hoomans everywhere. How can I be expected to patrol that entire place by myself!?! The mantle of responsibility was heavy, but The Hairy One and I rose to the occasion. I demanded we do potty and patrol breaks every hour or so all night. #AndAlsoBarkAtEveryVoiceOutsideTheDoor

On most patrols we would encounter hordes of teenage and other hoomans who squealed and rubbed my belly on demand. All I had to do was roll over, belly-up and those girls giggled and loved on me. Dozens of them took turns telling me how beautiful I am. #TheyWereSoRight I catalogued millions of smells just from the room and hallways. So many smells. #ILoveTheSmells

We went to my first party at Melissa's house in Williamsburg where I got to play with Juno and her pack of small hoomans. One small hooman called Sarah was a perfect size for sitting on. They had chickens in their yard, but I wasn't allowed to "play" with them. They looked delicious... I mean friendly. The hoomans said I was a very good boy and handled all the fun and noise well. I tried my best to manage all the hoomans and keep things under control, but I was outnumbered, and they wouldn't obey me. #ItWasMadness

We also entertained guests at my primary dwelling this week! Another nice lady (also named Melissa) came from a strange land called "New Jersey" with her hairy one and small hooman. Her hairy one gave me lots of scratchies and attention and she let me lick her face (that's my favorite). But at some point, the hoomans were ignoring me so I ate a hole in and swallowed a 6" section of blanket. #TheWorldRevolvesAroundMe When I eat foreign things it forces the hoomans to monitor my poop closely for days. And I find that to be an adequate punishment. #ItHasntComeOutYet

Last weekend the hoomans put my treats into strange plastic eggs, hid them in the yard, then made me go find them. They claimed a bunny put them there. #TheyArentVeryBright It was exciting but not at all efficient. Why don't they see that just putting the treats directly into my treat-hole is the fastest way? #JustTossThemRightInThere

I've discovered a wonderful new supply of grass. Daddy says they are lawnmower grass cakes. The only problem is I have to snarf quickly before the hoomans steal it from my mouf. They are delicious, crispy and muddy. #CheersToTheChef

Daddy took me for a play date with my friend Rex at the dog park. There were so many muddy puddles and Rex and I had a blast playing "chase me – no you chase ME." That was super fun, but the only picture daddy took was of me standing alone sniffing hay. #DaddyFail #AtLeastHesCute

The Squishy One prepared us homemade frozen yogurt and fruit treats while we were at our play date. After the horrid post playdate bath, Daddy and I settled in for some snuggles and frozen yogurt. It was a very busy week full of fun and adventure. #LifeIsGood

That's all the news and #Finnanigans from this week. Over and out.

Good morning, Mama. I'm just gonna lay on your chest and work on my nubby toy.

# Special Report
April 28, 2019, Part II ·

Finn here... working on my selfies. Help me pick one for my Bow-Wow dating app profile.

# Week Sixty
May 4, 2019 ·

HI, EVERYONE. FINN HERE with my week 60 report. After we drove home from our crazy night in Williamsburg last Saturday, we went to an expo called "Petapalooza" and it .... was .... epic!! I got to meet Nancy and jump up on the edges of her display tables which made my hoomans scream and jump to stop them from falling over. That was a fun game we played all day at the expo. The hoomans spoke to

one lady about agility training and she asked if I had completed "manners training." The hoomans seemed unsure how to answer, so I answered by jumping on her table and pulling down all the signage then jumping on her head when she tried to pick it up. #WhatTheBathIsMannersTraining #HowsThemMannersLady

I also got to speed date lots of other dogs as well as some kind of horse they called a "Great Dane." I must have kissed thirty other dogs in under an hour. What a rush. #LLFinn #BestKisser

A special small hooman kept following us around and asking to pet me. She was nice and smelled like candy. I was extra sweet with her because I could

tell she needed gentleness. I didn't jump on her and I sat nicely while she touched my face. She giggled when I licked her face and called me a "nice kitty." The hoomans were surprised by this and gave me lots of treats and love for being such a good boy with her. #IHaveMyMoments

But, best of all... I finally got alone time with my K9 Camp pack leader, Scott!!!! I always knew he loved me best but just couldn't show it in front of the rest of the pack. He gave me kisses and even put me in charge of the information table. I'm pretty sure I attracted some new ladies to join us for "chase me" time in the play yard. #NoCommissionNecessary

We left there and went to another new place they called "Uno's House." I got to meet Uno's hoomans- Ed and MaryLynn and I ate some of their lawn. MaryLynn played with me and scratched my ears. #MyFavorite

By the time we got home I was so tired I could barely walk. I refused to get out of the car and made The Hairy One carry me inside. #IHavePeopleForThat Then I slept for 4 straight hours and even forgot about dinner time. #OverStimulated

The Squishy One made The Hairy One some homemade ricotta cheese and wouldn't let me eat it all. I was so mad. #ItWasMagicallyDelicious So I guilted her into making me homemade dog biscuits the next morning before work. #PeanutButterIsLife #CouldveUsedSomeBaconThough #WrappedAroundMyPaw

I heard them talking the other day about how strange it is that I don't run to the door to greet them when they get home. I don't greet them at all. They have to come to me. This is all part of my dominance-management protocol. The Squishy One said she's not playing along anymore and tries to hold out until I come to her.
#LetsSeeWhoBreaksFirst

That's all the news and #Finnanigans from this week. Over and out.

# Week Sixty-One
May 11, 2019 ·

HI, EVERYONE. FINN HERE with my week 61 report. This week started out great. The Hairy One took The Squishy One somewhere and left her there!!! I can't be sure if it was by accident or on purpose. All I know is she packed her stuff into the wheel-boxes, they got into the go-for-a-ride, and he came home Sunday without her!!! I had him all to myself the whole glorious week. #ByeFelicia

We did everything together. Morning staff meetings were a little less fun, but we held our own. I helped him with his work, we went on long walks together, we even snuggled.

#BroManceWithoutInterruption

By mid-week though, I was realizing some problems with this new arrangement. For starters, I had no one to dominate. Second, I had no one sufficiently squishy with squish in all the right places on whom I could lay.
#DominatingIsOneOfMyFavoriteThings
#SheCallsItCuddling

I was gloating to the guys at day-camp and they pointed out that this makes ME the lowest member of the pack. #Unacceptable

I came home that day and decided it was time to challenge Daddy for pack leader status. I started with a very dominating pee in his office. I also got a bit more serious about our wrestling matches. #MoreBites

I think it was clear to us both that I'd become alpha. At least until dinner time. Then it all fell apart. My reign was short but powerful. I was a good and gracious leader. #DinnerRequiresThumbs #HeAlsoWorksTheGoForARide

When Daddy left the house on Friday night, I could only assume he was picking up another dog for the pack. A submissive and possibly squishy friend to boss around. But he returned with HER! He brought back The Squishy One!! She smelled of wondrous far away things. She smelled like she'd eaten a lot of avocados and said she had been in a place called California. Maybe she was at an obedience school for pack management – where hoomans learn to stop trying to be alpha.
#SheGivesHimLipSometimes

The next morning the hoomans surprised me with a trip to another dog carnival. I played in the off-leash area with so many doggies, I lathered up an excellent dognado, I played fetch with a small hooman, and best of all, found a shoulder-deep mud puddle and went for it. Face-first. Twice. #WorthIt

Then we walked around the carnival part and practiced "not jumping" on people. Much to my glee, both Scott and Amber from K9 Camp were there, and I got lots of special loving they can't usually give me in front of the pack. We all know I'm their favorite, but we have to pretend they love all the dogs the same. #YoureNotFoolingAnyoneGuys

I really enjoyed my special week with Daddy, but it's nice to have The Squishy One home and be the boss again. #IAlsoLikeDelegating


That's all the news and #Finnanigans from this week. Over and out.

# Week Sixty-Two
May 18, 2019 ·

HI, EVERYONE. FINN HERE with my week 62 report. I have only one important update this week and it may be THE most important intelligence I've ever sent back to HQ... so gather round. #Closer #CloserStill

I've discovered a foodstuff called a "pup cup" from a strange place the hoomans call "Dairy Queen." I had the same thoughts you're having right now... "Why would you want to eat a cup of puppy?" And "Why would a Queen give us her cup of puppies?" It's a lot to unpack. #ItWasntEvenAVeryNiceCastle

The "pup cup" didn't appear to have any puppy or puppy byproducts (Thank Dog!). It was very cold, soft yet firm, very lickable, sweet and delightfully creamy. It reminded me of milk from when I was a puppy – maybe that's the reason for the strange name. All I know for sure is that it was delicious!!! I mean bacon on a weekday, five-day-old fish and peanut butter delicious. I've never had anything so delicious. #DeliciousIsntStrongEnough

I was so enthralled that I was drooling while I was eating it. My spit got foamy around the edges of my mouth. I know this sounds like a reaction to poison, but it was just that glorious. The hoomans kept saying "slow down" which only made me lick faster. #TheyWereGonnaStealIt

I got half that evening in the car and then they stole the rest from me and took it home. #IKnewTheyWereGonnaStealIt I saw The Squishy One put it in the cold box in the kitchen when we got home. I prayed to the cold box all evening to give it up. I barked at it a while and even growled. But the cold box just stood there, silent and stoic. #BigJerk

At the Dairy Queen's castle, I saw a hooman dispense the frozen slop of all that is good in the world from some kind of machine. You must contact this

Dairy Queen and ask her for a machine for HQ. And since I discovered this for all of dog-kind, make sure to send one here to me. You have the address. #INeedMoreFrozenDairySlopASAP

I also investigated something called "raw cauliflower" this week and it's just awful. The Squishy One was eating it and I mind-ninja'd her into giving me some. I don't know how she eats that stuff. So far, I find all vegetables to be a waste of sunshine and water. Bleghk. #AndIEatGarbageSometimes #SoItsALowBar

Oh, I also had fun at camp three days this week, cuddled with my hoomans, enjoyed one of my better power naps, and had lots of walks at the park. But really.... find the frozen dairy slop machine. Let nothing distract you from this new mission. #ItsMagicInACup

That's all the news and #Finnanigans from this week. Over and out.

# Week Sixty-Three
May 25, 2019 ·

HI, EVERYONE. FINN HERE with my week 63 report. What a week! My hoomans surprised me Sunday with a date with Sedona. She's my favorite Vizsla from the Vizsla Meet-ups!! I don't know how my hoomans knew, but they arranged a play date for us at camp!!!!! It was two hours of pure magic. We ran, we chased, we growled, we chewed on each other, we played in pools, and even got to try some agility stuff. We had a private moment in the blue tunnel and Sedona told me a secret. Best of all my favorite hoomans were both there: Daddy and Scott. Oh, and so was The Squishy One and Sedona's hooman pack. #LivingMyBestLife

I also got frisky with one of my favorite hooman girlfriends at the vet. Her name is Abby and she always squeals with delight to see me. #WhoWouldnt It turns out my scary lump wasn't a histiocytoma after all. It was just a gnat bite combined with a bacterial staph infection. I have itchies all over, but I'm on medicine now and The Hairy One gave me a special bath with stinky shampoo to help. Dr. R. says I'm more susceptible to stuff than most dogs. #ImSpecial

We've returned to our alternate dwelling this week, and it's been one adventure after another. I found a snake skin, then its owner (a dead ringneck snake #RIPbuddy), and hunted some

jumpies my hoomans call frogs. One of the jumpies jumped up at my face, and I launched a foot into the air. Later that day, during our evening patrol, I found a bird up in a tree. I tried to get her to come "play" with me, but she refused, and daddy just tugged me away.
#DancingFinnNeedsATutu
#AnimalKingdom

Following up on my last report, have you made any progress on finding me a frozen dairy slop machine? I need it. I need it, bad! Please keep me posted as to how I can get more frozen dairy slop!! I've tried telepathy with the hoomans and they just aren't getting it. All day and night I dream about it.
#TheDairyQueenIsMissing
#LongLiveTheDairyQueen

The Squishy One says I get to have a long date with my #1 girlfriend Jessica today!!! I'm so excited. #ThereWillBeCuddling

That's all the news and #Finnanigans from this week. Over and out.

# Week Sixty-Four

June 1, 2019 ·

HI, EVERYONE. FINN HERE with my week 64 report. I got to go to another party last week at Lexi's house. Lexi was so sweet and pretty. I could tell she's an older girl and having some aches and pains. So I knew I had to be gentle and not jump on her to play. The Squishy One and The Hairy One were pretty surprised that I regulated myself, and they gave me lots of praise. Lexi and I still had fun though, and Lexi really liked me!! Her hoomans, Patti and Richie, loved on me and told me I was a good boy. Lots of other hoomans like Jyll and her small hoomans played with me and kissed me. I even got to eat some leftover burger off a little hooman's plate. It was a busy and overstimulating party. I was a big hit all around. #AsUsual #TheBestPartyHasLowTablePlates

The next day I was given a strange food stuff the hoomans called a "red bell pepper". It was horrible and worthless. I'm not ever sure it can be classified as food, but I did see the hoomans eating it. Why can't they understand I only like protein, peanut butter and dairy!? #BaconIsLife

I also enjoyed some productive domination of The Squishy One in our favorite chair. She calls this "cuddling," though I believe she knows better. #IMayNotBeAlphaButImNotCharlie

That's all the news and #Finnanigans from this week. Over and out.

# Week Sixty-Five
June 8, 2019 ·

HI, EVERYONE. FINN HERE with my week 65 report. I regret to report that the hoomans tried to kill me last Sunday. By my count, at least 6 times. They tricked me by telling me we were going to a Vizsla meet-up to see my friends. Of course, I was excited to go and chase everyone. #EspeciallySedona

But not long after arrival they hurled me ever closer to my death. They forced me into a very, very large bathtub with no bottom and tried to drown me. #WhereDidTheGroundGo

A woman dragged me to the middle of the strange bottomless bathtub. Then she let me go and told me to "swim" back to The Hairy One standing safely on the edge (where you don't almost die). I don't know what she meant by "swim," but while I was running for my life in the water, the idiot hoomans were cheering and praising me!? For what?! Not dying?! Meanwhile the nice lady was following me (see also, "chasing"), and pushing my butt up in the water which made my head go down!! I can only surmise her intent was to drown me!!! They did this FIVE times. At one point I attempted to save myself with a side-escape, but she caught me. #FoiledAgain

Once safely reunited with The Hairy One on the dock platform, I assumed I'd passed whatever torture test this had been. Perhaps I would get a treat to enjoy while being toweled off. But no. He walked me to a different bathtub with no bottom and tried to drown me himself! This time they

put me in a strange orange puffy vest that's frankly more of an autumn look, but whatever. The Hairy One tried to convince me to get in with him and when I refused, he snatched me from the safety of the dock platform and tried to drown me again. I was able to claw my way up his chest and clung to him for my life. #HeDidntAppreciateTheBearClawCuts #MaybeHeShouldntTryToDrownMeThen

And what was the idiot Squishy One doing during all of this? Taking pictures and videos! Cheering on my near-deaths and telling me, "You're okay, buddy." I mean, do I look "OKAY" to you in these evidence photos? #SheMustHaveBeenTheRuntOfHerLitter

Strangely, all my Vizsla friends were willingly jumping into and playing in these bottomless bathtubs. They all looked to be having such fun – retrieving toys and splashing around. Some even ran and jumped off a high platform, soaring through the air like Wonder Dog before crashing to their near death in the water. And then they would go back and do it again! #IDontUnderstand #MaybeImNotAVizslaAfterAll

With my trust entirely shredded and my faith in hooman-kind utterly rattled, we dried off and loped back to the car. I refused to give them any positive reinforcement for their bad choices. I laid with my back to them and refused any eye contact. I guess they decided extreme measures were necessary so they contacted the Dairy Queen to find out where they could get me some frozen dairy slop. It turns out, the Queen's jester had some... a clown called Ronald McDonald. I made clear that this bribe was offensive and wouldn't undo what they'd just done to me. #ButIAteItAnyway

I gave them the cold shoulder for two days, refusing eye contact, cuddles and tried my best to not even be cute. #WhichIsImpossible I threw several fits and screaming outbursts of profanity. They kept explaining it was meant to be fun for me. And the other dogs did seem to like it. So, I decided to forgive their transgression and make up. #AlsoTheyControlTheFood

I have been sharpening my antler into a shiv just in case I have to take them out in their sleep later. The Squishy One even holds it for me while I sharpen it. #Idiot

Later in the week, I helped them prepare a game they call a "scavenger hunt" for some little hoomans coming to see us next weekend. I helped wrap the treasure and found the perfect hiding spot. #ICanKeepASecret

They also gave me another strange food stuff called "spinach". I liked it ok – a lot better than the others so far. #TastesLikeGrass

That's all the news and #Finnanigans from this week. Over and out.

# Week Sixty-Six

June 15, 2019 ·

HI, EVERYONE. FINN HERE with my week 66 report. Apologies for my delay in filing this week's report. It's been a wild and wacky week here at Chez Finn. If I'm being totally honest, I forgot. It's been that busy and fun! #LivingMyBestLife

Last weekend, the 'rents abandoned me at home, and I wasn't feeling it. I put on a very loud protest concert and it must have triggered the security cameras, because within minutes, they were back – and mad. Apparently jumping up on the pool table for optimum acoustics is frowned upon. It's a good thing they came back though, because I was stuck up there. The Hairy One came inside and scooped me up (yay!), only to carry me to the penalty box (boooo!) for the remainder of their time outside. #Rude

Wednesday night, The Hairy One gave me an extra treat before nigh-nigh and boy was it a doozy. I remember a class on wacky tobacky, shrooms and other things we shouldn't eat, but I don't remember this. I was the sleepiest I've ever been and pretty dazed and confused for the whole next day. My back-right paw was getting uppity at times and the TV remote got downright belligerent. The Squishy One claims they "accidentally" gave me too much anxiety medicine while testing it out for the weekend with guests, but I'm dubious. #Sketchy #ThisIsWhyIHaveTrustIssues #WellNotJustThis

Thursday night was the highlight of the week! Melissa came back to see me and brought Daniel and all the littles. So many littles. I remember sitting on the littles at her house in Williamsburg. They love me and tell me I'm cute constantly. The tallest female little is trying to teach me to roll over, but I'm just teaching her to give me treats. We play and play, and they giggle a lot. It's so fun. #ILoveLittles

We did a scavenger hunt, played with Legos, and I've taught them how to properly adore me. #LLFinn #FastLearners

I'm off to get the littles to make me a Father's Day card for tomorrow. #Suckers

PS – Escargot isn't all it's cracked up to be in the movies. #FoundOutTheHardWay

That's all the news and #Finnanigans from this week. Over and out.

# Week Sixty-Seven

June 22, 2019 ·

HI, EVERYONE. FINN HERE with my week 67 report. Last Saturday we continued our fun with Melissa and the littles. I took them on a hike to the cove at James Farm Ecological Preserve, and we had a blast. We smelled so many glorious/horrible smells and saw magical/terrifying creatures in the water. Mattie showed me a particularly terrifying alien being she called a "horseshoe crab." I tried to warn her to put in down, but she wouldn't listen. We nearly died. #TheyNeverListenToMe I barked a lot to make sure everyone was safe in the big bathtub and to make clear to my hoomans not to force me in there. I may look terrified, but I'm not. I was just trying to save them! I'm not a scaredy-cat. #IKnowYouAreButWhatAmI

Sadly, my new entourage left on Sunday, just as I had gotten them trained the way I wanted. The littlest littles gave me near-constant affection and the taller little kept giving me treats for refusing to roll over. I could do that all day long. #NoYOURollOver #NiceTry

I had a couple nice days at the new playcare this week but came home with a tick bite and a dead tick on my inner leg. The Squishy One was not pleased about this. #TicksSuck #SeeWhatIDidThere

The hoomans caught an epic battle scene between me and a sky raisin on their "I'm watching you, stop it"

security cameras. They let me listen to the playback, which got me all riled up into another howling fit. Then they recorded my new howling fit. I don't know why my howling makes them laugh and hit "record."
#TheyAreSoEasilyAmused #ImJustTellingThemLikeItIs

I got to play with Richie and Patti on Thursday night when they came over for dinner. They are Lexi's hoomans. The Hairy One played with a bowl of wonderfully fishy-smelling raw shrimp over the trashcan that smelled so good, I drooled on the kitchen floor. I don't know why he was playing with them instead of eating them. The Squishy One ruined the whole dinner by cooking them. #PoorRichieAndPatti #ILikeMySeafoodStankyAndRaw

The Hairy One and I settled in for some quality Friday-evening snuggle time, but The Squishy One was so annoying. She just had to take pictures and interrupt our bromance time. She gets this way when The Hairy One pays attention to me. #JellyMuchMommy?

I'm sad to report it's been many sunrises since my last frozen dairy slop. I cry out with the song of my people, I beg, I look pitiful, I stare into their eyes and try to telepath my need.... but nothing has worked. Why must I be neglected this way? Please report back any progress on finding me the frozen dairy slop machine. #IFeelTheBurn #TheBurnForSlowChurn

That's all the news and #Finnanigans from this week. Over and out.

42

# Week Sixty-Eight
June 29, 2019 ·

HI, EVERYONE. FINN HERE with my week 68 report. This week was so boring. What a snooze fest. The only notable highlights were two days at playcare, wresting with Daddy and getting in trouble for injuring The Squishy One during fur-missile training. Apparently "That's hurts, Finn!" when I enter the room at mach speed and launch into her body like a fur-missile. #Whatever #SuckItUpButtercup

The hoomans just bang on their pooters and yack on the phone all day. They call this "werk." I call this "boring" and a major interference with ME TIME! I was forced to spend long stretches laying in the sun, napping on the bed, and patrolling the neighborhood from the front door. #AllByMyself #ISawFourBunnies

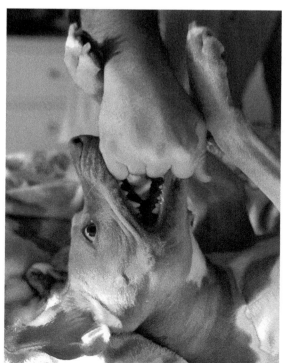

We did have a few solid team meetings this week. Lots of strategy this and task list that. I got another "talking to" from HR for sleeping on the job and chewing on The Hairy One all the time. But he shoves his hand in my mouf and I must cronch. #NoBites #IMustBite

My newest hooman-training tactic involves chewing on fabric. Clothes, bedding, blankets, whatever. It really gets the hoomans worked up in a lather. Well, mostly The Squishy One. Sometimes I can get The Squishy One to gasp and yell, "Nooooo... that's from Pottery Barn!" The hole in the "Nooooo... not the duvet cover, Finn!" led to the longest and most boring

discussion about how it's old and they may not sell it anymore... and the paint colors on the walls specifically match it.... and small holes can rip into bigger holes.... and blah blah blah. I love when they find a new little nibble-sized hole in something and lose their minds.
#GottaKeepThemOnTheirToes
#EveryBlanketHasAHoleNow
#ThatsWhatYouGetForLettingMeBeBored

The Squishy One took a thousand pictures of me doing nothing this week. I don't know why she does this. I mean, I know I'm gorgeous and all, but geez, lady, dial it back. And some are not very flattering.
#Rude #DoINeedBraces

That's all the news and #Finnanigans from this week. Over and out.

# Week Sixty-Nine
July 6, 2019 ·

HI, EVERYONE. FINN HERE with my week 69 report. This week was the worst!!!! No day care, playcare or play dates of any kind!!! The Squishy One says it's because it was a holiday week, so everything was booked. #ExcusesExcuses

My best girlfriend Jessica swung by for a quick bite one evening when the 'rents were out gallivanting with friends. That was definitely the highlight of my week!! #AtLeastJessLovesMe

It's been super-hot, so we can't even do long walks. I've been forcing The Hairy One on longer frog-hunts at 11pm and occasional neighborhood patrols at zero-dark-thirty to make up for it. #IReceiveNoAppreciationForMyFlexibility

Speaking of frogs, what does HQ have on file about these things? I need more Intel. They are curious creatures. They seem to like playing dead then abruptly jumping up at my face! I am then forced to spring equally far back and into the air (not from fear of course, but rather a proportionate-response battle technique.) They smell delicious but don't taste it, though they do taste better than the snails. #TrustMeOnThis

I saw Fergie in the neighborhood a few times, but we were both walking our hoomans on leash, so we couldn't go play. #IThinkSheDigsMe

The hoomans set up a very large water bowl on the back deck again and an elaborate trail of towels to protect my paws from the hot boards. They took me out there and I drank from the large bowl, but this didn't seem to appease them. The Hairy One then sat in the water bowl and tried to coax me to come in and play. I mean, he is delicious, but I have no idea why we had to go through all that just to flavor my water. I can just lick his face from inside the house. The Squishy One kept squeaking my toys in the water and bless her heart, splashing as if that would entice me. These hoomans have such strange rituals. #GoodThingTheyreCute

That's all the news and #Finnanigans from this week. Over and out.

# Week Seventy

July 14, 2019 ·

HI, EVERYONE. FINN HERE with my week 70 report. The hoomans have been hyper-focused lately on making me roll over on demand. I'm hyper-focused on _not_ doing that. But they keep at it. The only benefit is five minutes of extra treats each "training" session. #Suckers #ItsNotThatIDontUnderstandWhatYouWant

I discovered the joy of cronchy water this week. The Squishy One has a special machine that makes super cronchy cronch water nuggets and she shared some with me after a long hot walk. It turns out they aren't scary as previously reported. They are amazing!! They are treat-sized, cold and cronchy bites of heaven. Sometimes she puts them in my water dish, and I snorkel for them. #TheBubblesMakeHerLaughLikeAnIdiot

The Hairy One cooked some pink meat tubes on the outside fire and shared some with me. They were delicious. I was really loving this new foodstuff until I heard The Squishy One ask me if I was enjoying my "hot dog". #OMGDogsAreDelicious #ImACannibal

I scored two days at playcare near the alternate dwelling and even made the spotlight for their social media. They love the way I prowl the fish painted on the bottom of the baby pool. #ImFamous

The hoomans and I also worked on a jigsaw puzzle. They aren't very good at sharing or playing together though. Every time I tried to pick up a piece, they gasped at me and stole it right out of my mouf! Clearly, they rely on me for my supervisory skills and don't want me working side by side in the trenches. They also flipped out when I walked across the board. #Rude #ThatsWhyImMiddleManagement

We car-rided all the way back to the primary dwelling on Friday, but my tummy didn't like it. So, I threw up twice in the car. I was pretty mad that the hoomans pulled over and stole my food-puke! That's not fair. I wanted to save it for later. The good news is that I got to go see my friends at K9 Camp!!! They all missed me, and I missed them! #ImFamousHereToo

That's all the news and #Finnanigans from this week. Over and out.

48

# Special Report
July 14, 2019 ·

Peasant... why are you just standing there? Fetch me a treat.
#SideEyeWithASplashOfDisdain

# Week Seventy-One

July 20, 2019 ·

**HI, EVERYONE. FINN HERE** with my week 71 report. It's been soooo hot outside this week. Crazy hot. I got to go to K9 Camp on Monday and Tuesday - back to back fundays!!! I like playing in the baby pool and being supervisor in charge. My job is to make sure we don't have any "code brown" situations in the pool. I run a tight ship, and only certain dogs are allowed the honor. #NoCodeBrownersAllowed

We played fetch and ate frozen dairy slop in my play yard one evening. This frozen dairy slop wasn't soft and creamy like we get at the Dairy Queen tho. It was hard and took a long time to eat. #StillGood

The Squishy One loves the way I hop like a bunny when I chase a ball. She giggles like a fool and throws the ball just to see me do it again. #IThinkSheLikesMyButt

We went back to the alternate dwelling mid-week for reasons unknown. I like it there because I get more walks and get to see my neighborhood friends. I also like it there because the hoomans like it there. #ForShore #BeachVibes

I supervised The Squishy One at work on Thursday. I forced my way up onto the chair and squeezed in behind her. But she wouldn't share the headset, so I couldn't follow the conversation very well. I did my best to halp. #ImMiddleManagement

The only real downer for the week was a totally unnecessary, uncalled for, and undeserved bath. The Hairy One went in to take a shower and then forced me to get in, too! I was horrified. After it was over, I laid in a blanket swaddle in The Squishy One's arms, quivering to a degree entirely appropriate to the level of trauma. She held me and told me I was a good boy and fed me treats. #NextTimeIMightCodeBrownInTheShower

That's all the news and #Finnanigans from this week. Over and out.

# Week Seventy-Two

July 27, 2019 ·

HI, EVERYONE. FINN HERE with my week 72 report. We returned to the primary dwelling mid-week and I performed the customary perimeter check. The grass in my play yard has finally filled in enough for me to stop and eat while the hoomans try to make me chase a ball. #TheyHateThat

I got to go to K9 Camp 3 whole days this week! That was so much fun. #TheyLoveMe #WhoDoesntThough

Two strange creatures appeared in the yard while I Daddy and I were out on patrol. He called them "just deer" and said they

are friendly. I scared them away just in case. #NotOnMyWatch

The hoomans disappeared again. Terry came over and is taking care of me. I guess she knew somehow that they would abandon me. She is staying with me at home until we find them. Thank goodness she knows the precise order in which I must be fed, treated, and taken outside. I've trained her previously and she remembers! #SheLovesMeToo

I don't know what I'm going to do with these fools. I noticed they put clothes in wheelie boxes before they left, and this seems to correlate to these disappearances. #StillInvestigating

That's all the news and #Finnanigans from this week. Over and out.

# Week Seventy-Three
August 3, 2019 ·

HI, EVERYONE. FINN HERE with my week 73 report. The hoomans returned on Tuesday smelling of strange new and exotic places they called, "Cleveland." I was so relieved they were okay that I dropped my guard briefly, wriggling my whole body with excitement and knocking The Squishy One down so I could lick her face. We even cuddled a while with my head on her chest, until I remembered I was furious. Then I made a sharp left onto "you're dead to me" highway. After a few hours of side eye, pouting and angry glares, they gave me dinner and we made up. I may or may not have also eaten a new hole in the throw on the sofa to make clear my disgust. #ToughLove

Their time away made me realize just how lax I've been with their training. Having Terry here was a breath of fresh air and perspective. She is trained perfectly and does everything I want, sometimes even before I've thought of wanting it. I really did a good job with her and she's a top-notch employee. I need to redouble my efforts with these two hooligans before their performance sinks even lower. #TerryIsTheBest #TheyAreTheWorst

Speaking of poor performance reviews, see the enclosed video of The Hairy One claiming to give me a treat, but in fact doing the old bait and switch with some nasty, slimy, sweet thing they called a "peach." If you listen, you can

hear The Squishy One laughing as he taunts me with this vile fruit. Why don't they just give me the frozen dairy slop I love so much? Terry did.
#ILikeProtein #ThisIsNotProtein

We had a heated staff meeting yesterday and some accusations were made about "someone" eating all the snacks in the break room. They're not wrong, but I'm still offended.
#HRWasCalledInAgain

Last night we went for a mani/pedi at Dr. K's office. That was so nice. All the girls love me there, and Dr. K even sat on the floor loving on me while the girls cleaned up my nails. I love Dr. K the mostest. The Hairy One snapped one picture of me pouting when she left the room. I hate it when I'm not being lavished with attention.
#LLFinn

We also played in my play yard for a while but The Hairy One gets so mad when I stop playing to graze at the salad bar.
#ItsNotProteinButILoveHowMadItMakesHim

That's all the news and #Finnanigans from this week. Over and out.

# Week Seventy-Four

August 10, 2019 ·

HI, EVERYONE. FINN HERE with my week 74 report. It's been a tolerable week with these hoomans. On Sunday, we drove to the alternate dwelling and stopped on the way at a new park. I love new smells and things to explore. But I got pretty overheated and The Hairy One punished me by sticking me under a spray-mister thing. When that didn't work, The Squishy One put ice packs under my arms pits and on my belly. On my belly, people!!! You try it. #SheIsADevilWoman

Once she'd had enough of torturing me, we kept driving and eventually came to another Dairy Queen castle. She must have so many! I was delighted to get an "I'm sorry for putting ice on your nether bits" frozen dairy slop. #WorthIt

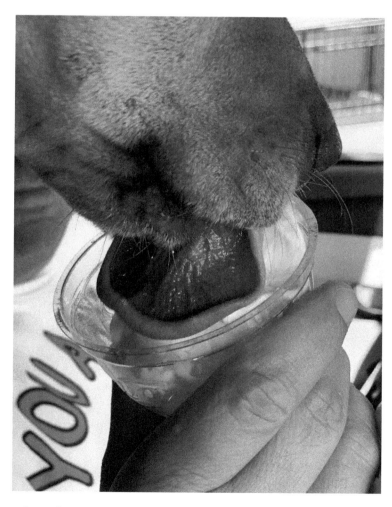

Upon arrival at the alternate dwelling, I performed my customary perimeter check and house inspection. The house inspection revealed no danger, but the perimeter check was a different story. I discovered and chased off a bird at least 7" big. It was, I believe, a robin. They are killing machines. I saved my hoomans and I'd do it again. #Everyday

Playcare was fun on Monday, but these idiots forgot to book any days the rest of the week (and it was full), so I was stuck at home staring at my toe beans. The Squishy One tried to help by giving me two new toys in one day. That was exciting, and I do love them. One is heavy and good for chewing, and the other one is big, soft and squeaky. It's shaped like a KONG but it's bouncy. #ItsNotJustTiggersThatLikeToBounce

It's gotten me wondering where dog toys come from. Who allots them? Who controls delivery? Who picks squeaky, soft, or stuffie? Why don't I ever get stuffies? I need to investigate the system and make some "process improvements." #NeedMoreStuffies

I did get a lot of extra walks this week. Towards the end of one walk we found a glorious rain puddle, and we played and splashed. Then we came home and played some more while The Hairy One tried to dry me off. I love that big guy. He's not very easy with the treats, but he's good on our walks and plays nice on the floor with me. #NoBites #IMustBite

On Friday, Rebecca and Max came for a sleepover!! They played with me and told me I'm the cutest #duh and I made sure to chaperone them. When Max tries to kiss her, I shove my face in between and lick him away. #NotOnMyWatch I wanted to go say hi this morning, but The Hairy One kept me on the leash so I couldn't bolt up to their sleeping platform and wake them with kisses. #MaybeTomorrow

That's all the news and #Finnanigans from this week. Over and out.

# Special Report
August 12, 2019 ·

Mama... why are you just sitting there? Play with me, devil-woman!

# Week Seventy-Five

August 17, 2019 ·

HI, EVERYONE. FINN HERE with my week 75 report. Last Saturday was a big day! My cousins AJ and Willow came over with Aunt Summer. Then more cousins came over that I hadn't met before! Michael, Steph and Sienna were so nice. Mike let me lick his face and we had soulful eye-conversations. They ate seafood on the deck without me, which made me mad. But everyone said I was a good boy. As per protocol, I chewed a hole in a blanket to show my displeasure. #ItWasAOneHolePunishment

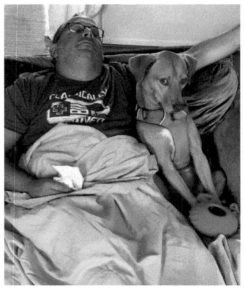

Things got weird Saturday night. The Hairy One started coughing and moaning. The Squishy One cleaned the house and put out bottles of something they call "Gatorade." I can only assume its lemonade made from alligators. The Hairy One went to bed and got very sweaty and weird. I remembered from my training that sometimes hoomans get the flu, and I realized this must be that. But I don't remember anything about alligator juice as a treatment. Then The Squishy One made him take a bath (the horror!) to break his fever. It became clear that I needed to help him since The Squishy One obviously had no idea what she was doing. #ILaidOnHisChestToHelp #AlligatorJuiceReallyMom #ABathNeverHelpsAnything

Rebecca and Max left on Sunday and gave me lots of kisses goodbye. I'm glad they left before they caught the flu. The Squishy One was sick by Sunday too, and then it was officially a full-on disaster. We're talking DEFCON 2. Who would feed me? Who would walk me and tend to my every need? #ILikeThingsJustSo #IHaveNeeds

As per protocol in DEFCON 2 situations, I had to decide which hooman I would save. The obvious choice, the only choice was my Hairy One. I spent all day Sunday, Monday and Tuesday on round-the-clock nursing care for him. I laid across his chest and snuggled his neck even when he was sweaty and whiney. I gave him my toys and my cuddle blanket. And I even brought him in a clump of grass from outside one morning. It was still fresh with dew. #DeliciousAndVitaminPacked

The Squishy One kept asking me why I wasn't nursing her and told me she'd remember this at Christmas. I don't know what that means but it can't be good. #ProbablyMorePajamasUgh

Thank goodness, The Squishy One took me to playcare on Wednesday. I really needed the break. It's exhausting taking care of a sick hooman. I got to play with my friends and burn off some crazy. But if she's well enough to drive me to playcare, shouldn't she be well enough to tend to my other demands!!??!! #IThinkSheWasFaking

I was sooo happy to see my best girlfriend Jessica appear at our door on Friday!! I was so tired from my nursing duties I didn't even remember we had a date. We went for a long walk and I told her all about the sick hoomans. #ThankYouJessILoveYou

Today seems a lot better for The Squishy One. She seems back to her old self and even played with me on the floor. #ImGladSheMadeItEvenThoughILeftHerForDead

The Hairy One is still coughing some and being generally pitiful. But The Squishy One says he doesn't have the flu anymore and now it's something called a "man-cold." I don't know what that is but I guess it means I'm still on nursing duty and subject to continuing awful service from these hoomans. #SendTreats

The Squishy One says I get to meet some new people today - including littles!!! I'm excited. I guess that's why she is bleaching all the surfaces in the house right now. #OrItsBecauseShesAWhackJob

That's all the news and #Finnanigans from this week. Over and out.

# Week Seventy-Six

August 24, 2019 ·

HI, EVERYONE. FINN HERE with my week 76 report. What a week! A lot to report. I've attached video evidence of my heroic acts related to the ceiling fan in the big room with our snuggling chair. It came on out of nowhere and I was the only one paying attention. I saved us all. #Again

The hoomans felt much better Saturday and proceeded to mess up the house by cleaning. The Squishy One said she had to kill the flu germs, but I think she just likes to taunt me with the vroooom vroooom, "it's just a vacuum, Finn" machine. #ItTouchedMyBed #IAlmostDied

Later that day Zaid and Giles came over with their three littles. They were fun! I scared the middle little when I jumped on him and licked his face without warning. But he was brave and let me lick his hand later. I love littles the best. #EasierToReachForLicking #StickierThanBigs

On Sunday, for reasons unclear to me, we returned to the primary dwelling. These long drives are exhausting. I was pleased to spend Monday at camp!! But then we came right back the next day!! What is this madness? #ImOverIt

The long drives did get me thinking that I need to refine my strategy for potty break stops. When we do finally stop for a break, I want a twenty-minute walk and they want a two-minute pee pee on-demand situation!! As you know, it's a delicate balance knowing how long I can prolong sniffing and exploring by withholding the pee pee, but not going so long that the pee pee window closes. The academy taught us that as long as we hold the pee pee, we get to sniff and walk. But sometimes that backfires, and I get stuck back in the car with a full pumper! #ILikeSayingPeePee

In related news, I also haven't mastered the photo "non-cooperation window." On the one paw, if I don't cooperate it lasts longer, and the pain of the process continues. On the other paw, if I do cooperate then she wins and thinks she's the boss. #ItsBothArtAndScience

I also got to see vet tech Abby and Dr. Richards Friday. I don't know why though. She looked at a little bump and told The Squishy One it's nothing. At least I got to go say hi. #ItsFunExceptTheTemperaturePart

This morning we went to the boardwalk to pee on stuff and get overstimulated by every person, sight, and sound. The hoomans kept asking me to heel, watch them and sit. They're hilarious. #IMostlyDidnt #HopeSpringsEternalHoomans

That's all the news and #Finnanigans from this week. Over and out.

# Week Seventy-Seven

August 31, 2019 ·

HI, EVERYONE. FINN HERE with my week 77 report. It was a pretty good week. I've finally taught the hoomans my rollover trick. I've trained them to give me treats for sit, down, and then rollover. Three treats for one trick!! I have to keep the challenge up in order to sustain this daily treat-game process. So, I've determined that willfully ignoring the down and rollover command exactly 34.768% of the time is the key. #Winning #ItsJustScience

We did have one pretty traumatic episode here this week. I don't know why, but The Hairy One betrayed me. A deep betrayal that I may never, ever forgive. He left the house for a walk and forgot me. He was carrying something in his paws then just walked right out the front door. WITHOUT ME. Ensuing protest attached for your records. I try not to raise my voice, but sometimes they have to be punished. #HowCouldHe

I was also forced to get loud when my bed was askew from the sunbeam one morning. Fortunately, The Squishy One has done well in her training and came running when I sounded the alarm. #WrappedAroundMyPaw

One of our evening patrols was stressful. I was trying to snag some extra crispy grass cakes off a recently mowed lawn, but Daddy wouldn't let me. He's all, "this isn't a buffet, Finn." "Stop it, Finn." You stop it ya big jerk! Extra crispy grass cakes are my favorite!!! I have also really developed a taste for the escargot, but he steals them right out of my mouth! #Rude #NeededALittleButterAnyway

I discovered that when I nose or pounce on a slug, they retract their heads inside their bodies somehow. I wait for their little faces to come back out, and I pounce again. I also discovered when I pounce on hoppy things it makes them jump and run away. That's so much fun. #PeekABOO #PouncingIsntJustForTiggers

We ran into our friend Kim in the hood. I loved on her. She loved on me. It was great. She was delicious. But her cat wouldn't come over to say hello. I begged and begged and wriggled my whole body with invitation. But Maple wasn't having it. #IllKeepWorkingOnHer

That's all the news and #Finnanigans from this week. Over and out.

# Special Report

September 4, 2019 ·

Yuth guyth, I goth a new toyeeeee!

# Week Seventy-Eight

September 7, 2019 ·

HI, EVERYONE. FINN HERE with my week 78 report. What a week!! Broccoli, slow dancing, a squishy-wiggle, new toys and betrayal. I took the hoomans to

Patti and Richie's house for an end of summer party with Jyll, Rick, and the kids. We had a great time. I did tricks and got treats, played with the puppy next door, got lots of lovins from everyone, too. #BackOffHesMine

I had so much fun that I barfed up all those treats when we got back to our house. I selected the bedroom carpet as the optimal place for throwing up. #CarpetAbsorbsBetter #PartyFoul

I was once again pressed into valor when The Hairy One and I encountered a terrifying squishy wiggle on our walk. As the video clearly shows, it leered at me threateningly as I took my power stance to examine its teeth. Its ferocity was clear, but I knew I had to protect The Hairy One. I barked and growled at it until it retreated. #ByeFelicia

Camp was fun this week except for one shocking betrayal. I had a lot of quality play time with Jameson and Sarah at camp. We chased, we chewed on each other and we wrestled. But one day a hooman came to get me from the yard. She took me inside and into a small room I'd never seen before. This room had a bathtub!!! I couldn't believe it. My happy place was infiltrated by a bathtub and the stench of betrayal. She violated me in the worst possible way. #NeedsMoreBubbles #TowelDryOnlyPlease #DryersAreTerrifying

I got a new yellow toy this week. It has a soft fabric outside and what I can only imagine is a

delicious pillowy inside. But the hoomans are keeping a close eye, so I haven't been able to get to the delicious insides yet. In return, I got a new stuffy bear toy for The Hairy One and I to share. We had a great time toying with it and making it cry for its very life right up until it met its maker. #ItsWhatWeDo #ByeBear

I also spent a lot of time cuddling The Squishy One this week. My allergies have been acting up, so I was extra pitiful and clingy. #SheLovesIt

I also experienced a new yum yum called "broccoli stem." It was a little hard for my tastes, but I made it work. #EverythingTastesBetterShredded #NeedsButter

That's all the news and #Finnanigans from this week. Over and out.

# Week Seventy-Nine
September 14, 2019 ·

HI, EVERYONE. FINN HERE with my week 79 report. Let's talk about treat management. As you know, here at Finn, Inc., I'm the VP of Yum-yums and accordingly, the Chair of the Subcommittee on Treat Management. I'm a very important furson in this organization. I've called several meetings to discuss the hoomans and what they call, "extra treats." (What does that even mean?) But my inputs are going ignored. #ThisWillNotStand

They take my perfectly wonderful, already accessible treats and shove them inside a torture toy. I am then expected to do work to get them out. I get very upset with the torture toys and scream until they come help me. This week, The Squishy One outright refused to help! A video of one negotiation is enclosed for your review. #Suboptimal

The Squishy One also had her barkday this week and there was so much annoying fanfare. First, The Hairy One tried to trace my paw onto the card in an effort to pretend I was into it. #IWasNot Second, a strange piece of mail came that I'm still trying to destroy. I watched her open it, some kind of card from Allison. At first it was fine, she smiled and seemed happy with the contents. But then, out of nowhere - demonic kitties were screeching out from the card meowing a barkday song! I immediately dove on the card to save her. She laughed and held me back from the kill. #ShesNotVeryBright

<u>I got into a regrettable disagreement with pink ball last night.</u> Things were said, and I regret my anger. In my defense, it was a full moon and my emotions are all over the place. #PinkBallBarelyEvenCared

The Squishy One has been all over me about my drooling during meal prep. I can't help that they take way too long to throw together just the right amount of two dry kibbles, sprinkle on the probiotic powder for my delicate system, and layer on creamy canned pumpkin purée to help control my booty juice. #ItsTheirOwnFault

That's all the news and #Finnanigans from this week. Over and out.

# Special Report
September 14, 2019, Part I ·

Boys meeting. #NoGirlsAllowed

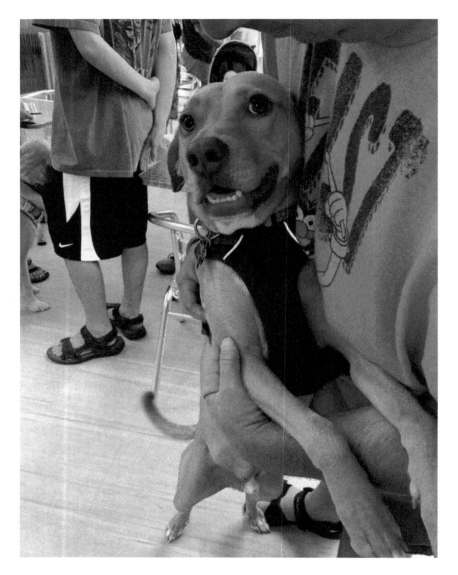

1. Is that ice cream!?!!!
2. Dad, Dad, it's icecreeeeeeem
3. Let's do this. . . I'll have two scoops for me and something for The Hairy One!

# Week Eighty

September 21, 2019 ·

HI, EVERYONE. FINN HERE with my week 80 report. I've discovered that the Dairy Queen doesn't control all the frozen dairy slop in the kingdom. I've also learned that some hoomans call it "ice cream." I know this because the hoomans took me to a place even more magical than the Dairy Queen's castle!!! It was called Salty Paws Ice Cream Parlor and Bakery for Dogs. It. Was. Incredible. Treats and bones and chewies and cookies EVERYWHERE. I did so much snifffffs. So. Much. Snifffffffs. Other dogs were there, too. The hoomans were pleased that we made it to the ice cream counter with only one knocked over display. I didn't have to pick it up

though, I have people for that. When we got to the ice cream counter, I realized what it was. FROZEN DAIRY SLOP. So many flavors and toppings. I picked peanut butter ice cream in a waffle cone with beef sprinkles and watched while the nice lady scooped it for me. The suspense was exhilarating. The Hairy One held it for me while I licked up the glorious slop. I even shared with a hot little number named Luna when some fell on the floor. The waffle cone was cronchy and I loved it. I loved all of it. The whole experience was extra amazing. I think my hoomans are finally starting to understand the level of service I require.
#Finally #ILoveCronchAndDairy

They also bought me a cookie shaped like poop with a smile face. I was confused. Why would poop have a face? And when I try to eat poop on our walks, they're all "No, Finn! Don't eat poop, that's gross." But if it has a creepy smile face they seem all in. #Weirdos #ButItWasYummy

We walked around town after our ice cream, and the smells on the sidewalk were glorious. Hot dogs, French fries, ice cream drips, cigarette butts, suntan lotion, candy drippings, seagull poop – a cacophony of all my favorite things. I even found a used baby diaper!! #ForTheWin

Later that day, The Squishy One made The Hairy One a treat. As she cut up raw tuna for his treat, she was throwing little tiny scraps into the magic bin of deliciousness. I stood watch, drooling as each piece went into the bin. Our eyes met, and she could tell I wanted it bad. And I could tell she was about to tell me no. In an instant, my instincts took over and I made the longest, widest swipe of my tongue that I could muster across the top edge of the trash pile. I scored!!! I managed to abscond with several juicy pieces of raw tuna. She chased me and yelled at me, but I did NOT care. It was delicious. It may have even been more delicious than frozen dairy slop!! #Sooooosh #WorthIt #SooshIsNowLife

I went to camp twice this week and got to play in the mud with Jameson both times. We love wrastlin' and chasing each other into as much dirt as possible. It was even caked inside my ear flaps.
#SpaDayMudBath #WeAreGoodAtIt

In unrelated news, The Hairy One gave me a horrid bath after camp both nights! Whyyyy does he ruin my amazing mud smell with stinky soap!? And then The Squishy One shoved little white sticks into my ears and stole the dried dirt I'd carefully left there.
#TheLittleWhiteSticksAreTerrifying
#IThinkSheTouchedBrain

Daddy disappeared one morning and did not return until nigh nigh. It was upsetting. And the dingbat Squishy One didn't even seem to notice. I tried to tell her how alarmed we should be and even politely waited until she was on a conference call. #SheWasntEvenGrateful #ISangTheSongOfMyPeople

She did manage to feed and walk me by herself. I was surprised. But she did not let me chew on her hands or bite her arms like The Hairy One does. Her service level was entirely inadequate. Especially now that I've experienced first class at Salty Paws. I tried later to convey my disgust with her via some of my best stank eye. #SheWasUnaffected
#OnceYouGoFirstClassCoachIsAwful

That's all the news and #Finnanigans from this week. Over and out.

Peanut butter is also life.

# Week Eighty-One

September 28, 2019 ·

HI, EVERYONE. FINN HERE with my week 81 report. Limes are weird and my paws hitting sand flips a crazy switch. These are my two major learnings this week.

In our ongoing series, "Finn vs. _____," The Squishy One offered me something she called a lime. It was strange. Firm yet squishy, juicy and fleshy, tart and sweet. #NotAFan

The hoomans abandoned me for what I can only assume was a trip to the doggy ice cream parlor and bakery. I'm convinced now that when they leave in the go-for-a-ride that must be where they are going. Why would they go anywhere else? I protested for some time with no impact. #Traitors

We returned to the primary dwelling and I performed my standard security checks upon arrival. Nothing amiss, I allowed the hoomans inside. #SafetyFirst

Shortly after arrival, I was pleased to receive an invitation to go... to... the... PARK!!!! I love the park. So many sniffs and other dogs. So many strange smells and stinkies. I don't know why the hoomans ask me over and over if I wanna. Of course, I wanna!! I think they just like to see my dance. #ItIsCuteSoIGetIt

Once at the park we stumbled on a patch of sand and just as my paws sank into the squishy ground, a surge of adrenaline shot through me. I was overcome with zoomies (which can be dangerous when I have the hooman on a leash). #Graceful I can only surmise this was triggered by the surge of terror and excitement I get when we go to the huge bathtub and I dig for sand crabs in the same sand substance. But there was no huge bathtub at the park. Just the sand. #Perplexing

I went to K9 Camp three times this week. #Winning But there's a new dog there they call Piper, and I heard Scott tell Daddy that "Finn met his kissy bandit match." I'll show them she's no match for me!!! #BackOffPiper #ImTheKissyBandit

That's all the news and #Finnanigans from this week. Over and out.

# Week Eighty-Two

October 5, 2019 ·

HI, EVERYONE. FINN HERE with my week 82 report. Well, The Squishy One left and didn't come back for a few days this week. I worried briefly but made a strategic decision not to really care and instead focus on my private time with The Hairy One. One morning while he and I were having our morning team meeting, a demonic voice started coming from that little black thing. I leapt to action to save The Hairy One from the demonic presence. #INosedItToDeath #NowImInChargeOfTheSupernaturalToo #YoureWelcome

Daddy took me to the sandy spot at the park, and we had super fun zoomies! I guess he caught my drift about how much I love sand, because that night we picked up Mommy in a loud and strange place she called "the big city." Then the next day I got to go to the realllly big sandy spot near the gigantic bathtub. #TheyreFinallyLearningHowToReadMe #SheSmelledLikeWorkMeetings

We had so much fun playing on the beach at sunrise and walking on the boards after. The beach had glorious smells and soft sand to dig. I found a mysterious, delicious confection Daddy wouldn't let me eat that Christa told Mommy was a whelk egg casing. I bravely charged the giant bathtub and dug in the sand. I jumped on Daddy and dragged him around with zoomies. It was awesome!! #BannerDay

Then we walked on the wood boards with all the delicious trash and food droppings! They made me get up on a chair to take stoopid pictures and I refused to cooperate. In retaliation, I ate a section of plant string sticking up behind me and Daddy went dental diving to steal it out of my face. #GetYourHandOutOfMyMouth #ActuallyILikeIt

That's all the news and #Finnanigans from this week. Over and out.

# Week Eighty-Three

October 12, 2019 ·

HI, EVERYONE. FINN HERE with my week 83 report. The good news this week is that Mommy trusted me with a crab stuffie last Saturday and I didn't kill it!! I got to carry it around and chew on it for five hours before the temptation overtook me. #MustDisembowel

The very bad, awful, no-good news this week is that the mysterious wheelie bags came out again on Sunday. Then Daddy dropped me off at K9 Camp and never came back!!! I don't know where they are, but it's been all week and they still haven't picked me up. I like playing with my friends, but I want to go home!
#ImTheKingThere #ItsGoodToBeKing #ThankDogForScott

Please send out some kind of search team for my hoomans!!!

That's all the news and #Finnanigans from this week. Over and out.

# Week Eighty-Four

October 19, 2019 ·

HI, EVERYONE. FINN HERE with my week 84 report. Well, ain't this some bathtub?! Those two idiots were fine all along. They showed up at camp on Wednesday like they had nothing to be ashamed of. The Squishy One captured my brief joy on video, but you can also see my disgust. I ran towards Daddy, initially overjoyed to discover he was alive then quickly shifting to furious that he chose to abandon me. Obviously, the dim-witted Squishy One had no choice but to obey The Hairy One. So, she can't be blamed for this betrayal. I can only imagine what she went through during our separation. #PoorDear #HeDidUsWrong #NineLongDays

In an attempt to comfort her, I've been relentless in my "suffocating love" strategy. If she's sitting down, I'm laying across her. If she's laying down, I'm

pushed against her or draped across her windpipe. If she gets up, I push behind her and wrap myself around her legs to make sure she feels me there as she walks. We had words in the laundry room because allegedly, "It's not big enough in here for that, Finn." #ItsAlwaysBigEnoughForFinn #IveMissedHavingSomeoneToDominate

The Hairy One tried to make it up to me with a long walk at our favorite park. But that wasn't going to sway me from my anger. He knew he was on double secret probation for his bad choices, and now he was trying to wiggle his way out of the consequences.

#ThisIsDefinitelyGoingDownOnHisPermanentRecord

I tried to play it cool... but then he took to me to the one place I can't resist. The sandy spot!!!!! I had my zoomies, I ran in circles while he tried to keep up, I tackled him. It's our thing. How could I resist our thing? He was forgiven. #Sandnanigans #ILoveSandWithoutOcean

Later we went back to the crib, and I showed him how much I love him in my love languages: bites and kisses. #NoBites #MustBites #TeethAndSpit #AllIsRightWithTheWorldAgain

That's all the news and #Finnanigans from this week. Over and out.

Mommy fell asleep before updating my online dating profile pic for me.
What do you think? I'm going for sultry but playful.
#ImIntoBitingAndLongWalksOnTheBeach

# Week Eighty-Five

October 26, 2019 ·

**HI, EVERYONE. FINN HERE** with my week 85 report. It's been a strange week as we adjust to being together again and I reestablish myself as Alpha. The Squishy One largely gave in and stopped fighting my love-smothering, but The Hairy One has maintained resistance. #IWillNotRelent #HeMustAssimilate

We went on a ride to a strange place that smelled glorious, like poop and lots of other animals. I had a great time sniffing around until we almost met our end. We encountered a strange beast they called, "It's just a baby goat, Finn." He was terrifying!! Lucky for him, he was behind a fence!! I was ready to fight him to save my hoomans, but Daddy pulled me away. We brought back strange orange orbs and dried corn products that they placed around the front elevation of the primary dwelling. These orange orbs smell just like what they put on my food every night. But the stoopid hoomans yelled at me when I tried to eat them. What the bark? They wouldn't even let me mark them so no one would take them. #FoodIsNotADecorationYouFreaks

They also took me back to K9 Camp a couple times this week. I was a little nervous they were leaving me again. It was great reuniting with the pack, and I loved playing all day, but I was super happy when they picked me up each night!
#ILoveCampButILoveHomeMore

A nice man named Jeff came for a sleepover! That was super fun. He let me lick his face and played with me. I found some old dog toys hidden in his guest room closet the day before. I stole a few before the hoomans noticed. #ImNothingIfNotStealthy

That's all the news and #Finnanigans from this week. Over and out.

# Week Eighty-Six
November 2, 2019 ·

**HI, EVERYONE. FINN HERE** with my week 86 report. What a week! This report will be an unparalleled roller coaster of emotion and news, just like my week.

We begin on a normal Saturday. The freaks woke me up with treats and forced me into yet another embarrassing costume. I was horrified at first and confused why they were putting bird feathers on my head instead of eating them. Then Daddy put on a costume, too!! WE MATCHED!!! My dreams came true - my bestie above the restie and I matched. We were twinning and let's just call it like it is -- we were winning at life. Not sure why Daddy was #1, though, when I'm clearly #1 in real life. #OKIllPlayAlong We even walked around the neighborhood for everyone to see us. Unfortunately, The Squishy One kept interrupting for photos and ruining our vibe. #ShesJealous #ShesNumberThree

Then, as if that wasn't amazing enough... I took the freaks to the giant bathtub! We played in the sand, dug for crabs, and frolicked in the frothy waves. It was heaven. Daddy and I even chased birds together. Lots of littles were also dressed in costumes and gave me lovins. Sometimes I was fast enough to shove my face into their bags of candy before anyone could stop me. I did have to save their lives from an ugly scary monster on the boards though. #IWasntAfraidHeWas

And because Mommy said I was already at "he's gonna need a bath" level of dirty, we decided to swing by the bay on the way home. I love the bayside almost as much as the giant bathtub side. So many smells, horseshoe crabs, and stinky bay plants. #TheSmellierTheBetter

We came home and while I was trying to enjoy a nap, these fools were doing some weird stuff with orange orbs. I tried to participate but they refused my help. The insides of the orange orb smelled exactly like the delicious orange slop they put on my kibble at dinner. #MmmnnFiber #ItWasAMagicalPerfectSaturday

The next day is when things turned awful. It happened again. Daddy disappeared with wheelie bags, but this time he left the dim-witted Squishy One for me to manage by myself!! It was a nightmare. You cannot imagine the stress from being pack leader *pro tem* when primary pack leader is away. I have to watch The Squishy One like a hawk, remind her of my every need and how I like them fulfilled, and make sure she knows about the ghosts near the window at 2:37 a.m. I spent most of the week jamming my snout into her neck or draped across her chest so she'd feel safe. I even supervised her in the tub. Normally, I wouldn't set foot in that room, but she was alone in the bathtub! I felt awful for her. Poor dear did it to herself. #SheCantHelpShesStoopid

During one of our walks (which she doesn't do right at all), a gigantic bird swooped down in front of us and nearly

carried her away. I scared it off up onto the neighbor's roof. She kept droning on that "It's only a Heron." Yeah, only a heron that nearly ate your face off, devil woman. #Idiot #YoureWelcome

She's lucky I saved her because the week was filled with her not doing things right. She goes the wrong way on our walks and doesn't even let me eat snails. When I pee, she carries on like a weird pee pee cheerleader. She didn't layer my food right and wouldn't let me bite her when we played. She said "no bites" in this weird tone of voice like it meant I shouldn't bite. It was madness. #ImAFiveStarDogLivingInATwoStarWorld

She also tried to roofie me one night "so she could get some sleep." She told me that my constant hanging on her neck and breathing hot air on her face was causing her sleepless nights. She gave me some extra "treats" at midnight and tucked me into my bed. I woke her around 1:30 a.m. standing over her like a scene from "Children of the Corn." I then spent the next hour explaining my disgust at her betrayal, barking at the ghosts and hanging on her neck. #SheDidMeDirty #AndItDidntEvenWork

Thank Dog, Daddy returned triumphant last night. I was so worried he was never coming back and I'd be stuck taking care of this hot mess forever. #SheIsATwoCaretakerLevelHotMess

That's all the news and #Finnanigans from this week. Over and out.

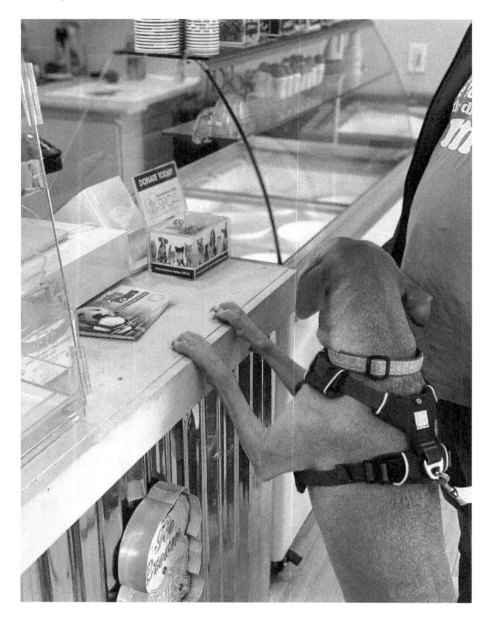

Yes, I'll take a double scoop of peanut butter chunk with tripe sprinkles, please.

# Week Eighty-Seven
November 9, 2019 ·

HI, EVERYONE. FINN HERE with my week 87 report. It was a solid week at the castle. Lots of adventures and napping days in between camp days. #ThePerfectCombo

Last Saturday was perhaps one of the best days of my life. It started back at Salty Paws for some ice cream and bakery items. After a pre-approval taste test on the cutest little spoon, I ordered a double scoop of peanut butter delight with tripe sprinkles. After the dairy slop I let the hoomans buy me some yogurt treats and a new antler. I just love it there so much. #ItsTheMostWonderfulPlaceInTheWorld #OnlyKnockedOverTwoDisplays

Then the hoomans took me to the boards and beach for a stroll. I love it there, too. But this time we stopped for breakfast at the Turtle Beach Cafe. A nice lady gave me a superb butt massage while the hoomans rudely ate

without me. And the owner, Tony, came out to give me lovins. I guess he heard the commotion about my cuteness all the way from the back. While we were exchanging kisses and love he snuck me not one, but TWO full size strips of delicious bacon!!!! I love that guy, and I tried to pull us back there the rest of the day. #IGaveThatPlaceFiveStarsOnYapp #TonyIsMyBaconDealer

I found a link to nine homemade dog treat recipes online and explained to The Squishy One that we needed to get on that, *stat*. She feigned refusal for a couple of days but eventually caved.

#IveGotHerWrappedAroundMyPaw
I'm thinking we should try one a week until Christmas and then decide our favorite. #SolidPlan Our first batch was a peanut butter, honey, blueberry, oatmeal number, and it was delicious! I even shared them with some of my neighborhood pals. The Squishy One made some in the shape of a squirrel and laughed and laughed. #SheThinksShesFunnySoIGoWithIt

The Squishy One was spending a lot of time working on some strange project from bed. She had a large wooden board set up with a thousand little pieces she was putting together in some specific order. She explained it was called a puzzle and said I couldn't halp. #Rude I have no idea the purpose of this task, but it was distracting her from me and making the homemade treats. I already have to share her attention with The Hairy One and her computer!! I couldn't allow another competing interest to infiltrate. After careful recon and terrain analysis, I decided a kamikaze fur-missile deployment was my best option for

attack. I started my run from the hallway to build up sufficient speed for launch. Then about three feet from the edge of the bed, I took flight. Mid-wind, I heard her scream, "Nooooooo Finnnnnnnnnnn!" but we both knew it was too late for her and that stoopid puzzle. Those pieces went flying and so did the cuss words. #MissionAccomplished

I went to camp twice this week. The first day Jameson and I got super muddy, so it ended in a hosing down. #NotIdeal The second day was delightfully hose-free for me and my buddy George. #Ideal

We did have one new issue creep up this morning. It's really my only complaint in an otherwise solid week. During my morning potty, I was doing my normal thing when out of nowhere, The Hairy One stole my pee! #WhatInTheBathtub It's bad enough they steal my poop, but now my pee, too?! I don't know if this has anything to do with me emptying my entire bladder into my bed the other night or having to pee every few hours lately. I don't like it. I hope this doesn't become a thing. #Freaks #PeePeeThief

That's all the news and #Finnanigans from this week. Over and out.

I belieeeeeeve it's past time for dinner, devil woman. I am displeeeeeeased.

# Week Eighty-Eight

November 16, 2019 ·

HI, EVERYONE. FINN HERE with my week 88 report. What can I report this week? No major breakthroughs on the hoomans' training to speak of. I did see some action during a night patrol. A very large woods-dog came running past us in the yard, and while I was busy saving his life, The Hairy One was saying, "It's just a deer, Finn." Ya, well you're a dear, too, Dad, but that woods-dog almost killed us. #DimWitted

The Squishy One is back to protesting my love-launches into her body. She claims it hurts when my paws hit her doing 25 mph and she yelps. Wah wah wah! What a baby. I'm a fur-missile of love and she's gonna come to love it. #JustYouWait

We've also switched to my fall wardrobe and I'm feeling it. They finally got me a properly fitting cable knit turtleneck that aligns to my stature in society. There are some pictures of me in it from when I had to get ugly with The Squishy One over a very late dinner. She, of course, took pictures instead of feeding me! #SheWasFourMinutesOverdue #ICantLiveLikeThis

They're back to another weird hobby I thought we'd done away with... toofscratching with tongue frosting. Every couple of nights, they pull out a strange stick and put delicious frosting on it, then scratch my toofs with it. They are so strange. I try to show them a much easier way to give me the frosting is by biting the tube and licking it off the stick, but they refuse to even try my process improvement. I got tired of the foolishness and bit the stick so hard it broke in my mouth. Then Daddy had to throat-dive for the pieces. I do love throat-diving with Daddy. #Cronchy

Last night we threw a party the hoomans called a "bonfire." There were lots of people here and yummy foodstuffs. I got to smell the smoke and get really close to the fire. And I got to play with my little buddy, Tristan. He's a little hooman I quite like. #HeTellsMeImPerfect #HesRight

Daddy and I had some bro-time this morning. I love it when we sleep in and I get to chew on his hands and nose from the comfort of our big bed. He pretends not to like it and I do it more. It's our thing. The Squishy One tries to cut in cuz she's jealous, but I can usually side-eye her away. #BackOffHesMine

That's all the news and #Finnanigans from this week. Over and out.

# Special Report
November 21, 2019 ·

It's well past dinner o'clock and despite my clear warnings, The Squishy One is just refusing to comply. I hope I survive this long enough to file a formal complaint in my Saturday report.

# Week Eighty-Nine
November 23, 2019 ·

HI, EVERYONE. FINN HERE with my week 89 report. Things have taken a decidedly awful, no-good, terrible turn. I don't know what's brought it on, but the hoomans have regressed terribly. They're disrupting all the habits and systems I've put in place to establish and maintain my role as ruler of the castle. Things have utterly fallen apart. I'm no longer allowed to jump up on the bed or couches without permission! I have to let them walk through doors before me and they're being sticklers about the "hoomans first" on the stairs rule. I was even forced to sleep in my bed on the floor – TWICE. I fought that one pretty hard for several hours with frequent "I need a drink of water," then "I have to go potty" attempts at interrupting their plan. #IAskedForStoryTimeAndWasRefused

"No more fur-missiles, Finn," and "You don't listen to my commands, Finn." Oh, and my favorite this week, "You're so willful, Finn." This is mayhem. The Squishy One says I've gotten too big for my britches and need to be reminded who's boss. She said, "Boundaries make for better buddies". #IAmTheBoss #PleaseFindOutWhatBritchesAreAndSendMeBiggerOnes

I'm unclear as to whether it was part of the "britches" situation or just a bout of moron-fever, but one night The Squishy One failed to feed me on time. She just sat there well past dinner o'clock with no remorse. I deployed all the usual tactics to remind her: distant stare down from my designated "hungry place," closer stare-down from a few feet away, very close stare-down from a few inches from her face, chuffing and pouting, pawing at her arm, and I'll admit even a little crying. This went on over 4 minutes, and I became so weak that I collapsed. The starvation was overcoming me, and I thought it would be the end. When she finally did feed me, a surge of adrenaline was the only reason I was able to get to the bowl. #IFiledAFormalComplaintWithHR #ThisIsGoingDownOnHerPermanentRecord

It's been really cold here lately, so I'm back to my fool-proof "Mommy's skin is warm and can heat up my icicle nose" system. I run back inside from potty time, immediately jump on her and press my cold nose against her skin. It's extra fun when I do it after our midnight pee pee patrol and she's sleeping. #ILikeTheSquealSheMakes #DaddyTellsHerHesSorryButHeIsnt

We're also back to my sweats and PJ's now that it's freezing around here. I love how soft and warm they are, and Mommy says all the ladies love them. #LLFinn

The highlight of the week was a surprise package from Susan! She sent me a hedgehog stuffie and very pretty keychains with my picture painted on them! Mommy says there's also bubbles in there we're saving for a snow day. I can't wait. #WhatsABubble #TeamSusan

The Squishy One wasn't feeling well yesterday so I tended to her diligently. Despite her insolence this week, it's my sworn duty as her primary care nurse. I stood on her chest, licked her face and slept with my face tucked as far under her chin as possible for maximum fur-to-skin surface contact and of course to monitor her pulse. I refused to get off her no matter how many

times she asked, and I suffocated her with my body heat to help her fever. #ImReallyGoodAtThis

I'm working on my retraining/retaliation to get things back under control. This morning I refused to go on sunrise pee patrol until after 9 a.m. #ThatllShowEm

That's all the news and #Finnanigans from this week. Over and out.

# Week Ninety

HI, EVERYONE. FINN HERE with my week 90 report. If she says "boundaries" one more time, I swear to Dog I don't know what I'll do! The Squishy One continues her ridiculous attempts to control me, and I continue my valiant resistance. #FinnStrong #VivaLaResistance #OneDayMore #246OOOH1

We did have a lot of fun this week, though. Last weekend I took the hoomans to a new pet store to look for some new threads. We saw a sweet kitty there who rubbed noses with me and told me how to get the workers to give me treats. #WinningAtLife

Then we went to camp! Well, sorta. We went to where camp normally is, and my BFF Scott was there like usual. But nothing else was usual!! Our playroom was full of hoomans and tables and we had to form an orderly line waiting to see Santa Paws. It was mayhem. I got to wait in line with my boxer pal Piper and we got to make fun of our hoomans while we waited. An embarrassing hat was shoved on my head, and then I got in to see the big guy!! I wasted no time running up to Santa Paws and telling him I want a kitty for Christmas. I also asked him to make The Squishy One stop with all the "boundaries" stuff. He said it was for my own good and I said nuh-uh. Then I gave him my signature aggressive face-lick-love and he gave a good laugh. #HeTastedLikeHappiness #ILoveSantaPaws

While on patrol in the sunroom I found a strange bug that looked like a warrior shield. I pounced on it (per protocol) and it let out a terribly stinky spray. My only choice was obviously to eat it. Surprisingly, it tasted terrible, just like the spray. Someone get a warning memo out to the others. I liked the cronch but regretted my decision immediately. The smell was all over me and in my

moufs. I ran to The Squishy One for help. But as soon as she smelled me, she screamed and threw me off her lap. #Rude #StinkBugsStink

We returned to the alternate dwelling, and I got to go see my friends at daycare. Only problem is someone there has been snitching on me!!! When I got home, the hoomans had a long (boring) talk with me about humping my bestie Jameson, air-humping when Jameson isn't available, and breaking into someone else's run and eating their breakfast. They sent a video! UGH! #IWasHungry #ImAlwaysHungry #SnitchesGetStitches

On Thursday we went to Patti and Richie's house! I got lots of love and yummies while we watched football. Best of all, they made two whole turkeys for me! When one turkey came out of the deep fryer, I jumped up on the dining room table to check it. Everyone screamed and lunged towards me like idiots. It was awesome. Their table was see-through and that made things more amazing. A delicious ham was up there and occasionally some made its way to me. I monitored things through the glass table just to make sure it was safe. I got to play a lot with Richie and we even took this cool picture of me standing on his feet! #ThankfulIndeed #ILoveRichie

That's all the news and #Finnanigans from this week. Over and out.

# Week Ninety-One

December 7, 2019 ·

**HI, EVERYONE. FINN HERE** with my week 91 report. The hoomans have relented in the great stuffie fight of 2018-2019. I've worn them down. It appears as long as I don't swallow the innards, I'm allowed to disembowel them. Interesting. Also, my new octopus one is the best. It has four squeakers and one kinda screams as the air lets out. I've

really enjoyed getting right in Mommy's face and letting 'er rip. #EspeciallyAtSixAm #ItStillHasSevenLegsLeft

I took the hoomans back to the boardwalk to find my special friend with the kisses and bacon. If I sit in the doorway of Turtle Beach Cafe and howl, Tony will sometimes come out with kisses and FULL SIZED pieces of bacon. Not broken up like other slackers give. This is a man that understands my stature and importance. There's nothing like eating full-sized, glorious strips of salty goodness while a nice man scratches your ears and tells ya you're cute. #WinningAtLife #TeamTony #TurtleBeachCafe

Sadly, that's the end of the good news for this report. The Hairy One dropped me off at camp on Monday and disappeared. The Squishy One picked me up that afternoon but he was nowhere to be found. I was alone to supervise her... again. She requires so much management and coddling when he is gone. It's crazy. I am also required to stay awake at night and bark at all threats, real or perceived. At 2 a.m., there is mandatory barking at ghosties. At 3 a.m. I have to growl at the spookies near the window. And at 3:40 a.m., there is a required possible intruder melt down. I try to climb on her head and keep my nose pressed into her neck as much as possible, so she feels comforted. Honestly, it's exhausting. #ItsHardToBeKing #WhatWouldSheDoWithoutMe

The only bright spot during these dark days was a rotting, smelly, steaming dead body I found on our walk. I was able to throw myself down and roll in it before The Squishy One even knew what was happening. It was glorious. I'm not sure what it was… maybe something in the tree rat family. #Sucka #GottaBeQuickerSlowPoke

I really enjoyed listening to her squealing and cussing until I realized this was gonna end in a bath. #StillWorthIt

She has also persisted with the "boundaries" and dominance business. I've mostly yielded this week, since she is clearly hysterical and helpless without our pack leader. #PickYourBattles #SureHoomansGoThroughDoorsBeforeDogs #KeepTellingYourselfThat

Daddy returned last night and, in the process, performed a surprise audit of my safety management skills. He snuck into the house in the wee small hours like an intruder to see if I would save the weaker, dumber Squishy One. #IDidnt #TheresAReportToCorporate #NowThereWillBeMeetingsAboutIt

My official portrait with Santa Paws came today, and I think I look exceptionally regal. I've attached a signed media release so you can use it for the Academy's holiday magazine cover. The younger recruits might enjoy seeing the level of regal to which they should aspire. #IAmACountAfterall

That's all the news and #Finnanigans from this week. Over and out.

# Special Report

December 12, 2019 ·

What do you mean it's time to get up!?!?!

# Week Ninety-Two

December 14, 2019 ·

HI, EVERYONE. FINN HERE with my week 92 report. It's been a ruff week. The hoomans have been willfully insolent and difficult. It's as if all my hard work in training them has been for nothing. And they persist with this "boundaries" stuff. For example, I finally got my learner's pawmit, but they won't let me drive! I hopped into the driver's seat while The Squishy One was loading up to go somewhere, and we had a pretty big fight about it. She's all, "You're not coming, Finn." And I was all, "You're lucky if I let YOU go, devil woman!" I held my ground, refusing to relinquish the seat until she

made it beep and move with some evil sorcery. #NotTodaySatanNotToday

We drove back from the alternate dwelling, and I repeatedly expressed my frustration with not being allowed to drive. After a while, The Squishy One started arguing back, but her command of Doglish is terrible. I tried to tell her she was talking nonsense, but she wouldn't listen and things escalated. Fortunately, The Hairy One hit record so I am able to attach audio proof of her idiocy. #ShesToneDeaf

The Squishy One faked sick on Monday and Tuesday with a fake sick she called a "migraine." It was clearly an elaborate ruse to avoid her responsibilities to me! I didn't even get cuddles!!! And The Hairy One kept locking me out of the bedroom so I couldn't jump on her head which obviously would have helped. #ImMedicallyTrained

The hoomans have also been trying to look inside my mouf for a couple weeks. I thought after the third toofsbrush I cronched in half, they would stop. There were several different attempts this week at getting me to open my mouf so they could look inside. Obviously, I refused. The Squishy One claims my breath stinks lately and my gums bleed sometimes. Sounds to me like the one who smelt it dealt it. #WhoHasBoundariesNow

Yesterday I got to go see Shannon and Dr. K at Yellow Springs Veterinary Clinic and they wanted to see my chompers, too! I love Dr. K so much! Just to mess with the hoomans and remind them who's in charge, I sat pretty for Dr. K and opened wide when she asked! I looked right at The Squishy One while it happened to make sure she was annoyed. #SheWas #WhosDrivingNowSatan

That's all the news and #Finnanigans from this week. Over and out.

# Week Ninety-Three
December 21, 2019 ·

HI, EVERYONE. FINN HERE with my week 93 report. It's been crazy cold but not a bad week overall. The freaks put another fake tree in the house and covered with it lights and dangly things I'm not allowed to play with. This appears to be some kind of annual tradition inexplicably connected to Santa Paws. The imposter tree doesn't even smell like a tree, and no one has peed on it. I don't know how they are so easily fooled. They also dragged out strange silver-colored fake deer from the shed and put them into the flower bed. The Squishy One tied ribbons on their necks and positioned one like it was eating and the other like it's a lookout.
#GoodLuckBlendingInShinyDeerWithBowTies #TheyAreTrulyMorons

The dangly things are so tempting though. A few of them are right at my face level, but I think I could pretty easily pull the imposter tree over to get to the others. #ImCalculatingTheWorthItQuotient

I went to camp and played so hard that I couldn't hold my head up when I got home. I just climbed into The Squishy One's lap and that was it. The hoomans call it "K9 Camp Coma," and they seem to enjoy it. They took a picture of me sleeping instead of fixing my squished snout. #TheyCantBeTrusted

Come to think of it, they take a lot of pictures of me sleeping. I've done some light internet research and that appears to be the behavior of serial killers and stalkers. So that's worrisome. #SleepWithOneEyeOpen

Daddy took me to the park for walksies, but it was so cold! I did some zoomies on the imposter beach area and played bucking bronco. I peed on stuff, and then we came home. He never pees on stuff during our walksies. #Weirdo

Last night I got a present in the mail from Debbie and Rico!!! And it was delicious!! Mommy let me lick the box, lick the tissue paper and then get my own treat out of the bag!!!! #WinningAtLife #ButSheWouldntLetMeEatTheRibbon


That's all the news and #Finnanigans from this week. Over and out.

# Special Report

December 24, 2019 ·

Trazadone and Mommy holding me like a baby make things better. I'll be napping here in her arms for the next two weeks if you need to find me. She says her arm is numb, but that sounds like a personal problem.

# Week Ninety-Four

December 28, 2019 ·

HI, EVERYONE. FINN HERE with my week 94 report. Santa Paws broke into our house! I'm both excited and disgusted with myself. I love that he left me treats and prezzies, but I obviously failed my pack by not protecting the dwelling from this intruder. He breached the perimeter, and I didn't even hear him! I gave no warning to pack leader and did nothing to scare him off. I've been told there were likely also gigantic reindeer creatures here, too. I saw nothing. I smelled nothing. How can this be!?!? #SantaSorcery #WhyDoesHeBAndE

Earlier this week I went to daycare and came home to a party!! Uncle Al, Aunt Summer, AJ and Willow were all here just to see me! We put stuff in boxes to make care packages for soldiers. I performed quality control to make sure there were dog treats in every box for the local village dogs and also the dogs on deployment. I accidentally stepped on some plastic air pillows and the pop scared me so much I counter-

110

attacked. I was a very good boy during hooman feeding time, and I got to cuddle with Willow a lot. I also got to open an awesome fake chipmunks in a fake tree prezzie. #FakeIsStillFun #ThanksSantaIntruder

But that's where the party ended. After the extra hoomans left, my hoomans noticed I was limping. We went to see Dr. K the next morning and she told us I tweaked my shoulder. Then she said the worstest, most awfulest thing -- no daycare, playing or exercise for two weeks. Two weeks!! No zoomies, no fur missiles, no sandbox crazies, no Daddy wrestling, no long walks, no nothing. Daddy says two

weeks is 14 days. Today is day five, and I'm already losing my mind. I spent the first couple days snuggled up with Mommy getting treats and cuddles just for being pitiful. Then I moved on to angry and frustrated. Now I'm moving into the "I will get you back for this" stage. I'm weighing my options for retaliation via jigsaw puzzle. The Squishy One has spent far too much time on that instead of me! Do I eat just one piece when she isn't looking? Do I jump up and "accidentally" slide across it? Maybe a few "almost accidentally wrecking it" moments to keep her nervous and afraid of when the next attack might come. #PsychologicalWarfare

The hoomans have also been making fire every night on something they call a Menorah. The Hairy One talks funny and then lights one candle at a time. Apparently, I'm not allowed to halp with that either! #Rude #ButTheCandleLightIsPretty

That's all the news and #Finnanigans from this week. Over and out.

# Week Ninety-Five

January 4, 2020 ·

HI, EVERYONE. FINN HERE with my week 95 report. After the shock of the Santa Paws B&E, we returned to the alternate dwelling for some R&R. It was nice to have new scenery for doing more NOTHING. I was still on exercise limitations (allegedly) because I (allegedly) hurt my shoulder. I think they just didn't wanna walk me or let me have any fun with my friends. I started to really crack up around day 10 of no zoomies, no walksies, no camp, no daycare, no fur missiles, no turbo digging, and no bird chasing. Things were getting bleak. #LazyHoomans #OperationRetaliationCommenced

After some well-executed retaliatory strikes, the hoomans finally relented and took me to the boards for a walk. We got to see lots of other hoomans and doggos. I dragged them immediately to the cafe where Tony, my bacon guy, lives but he didn't come out to see me. Then I took Daddy into the sand to bark at the gigantic bathtub and the white sky rats. We met back up with Mommy on the south end of the boardwalk when she heard me screaming at people passing by because they didn't stop to pet me. #Unacceptable Later we met a big doggo the hoomans called a Weishla. He was a big galoof but we got along ok. He was pretty pawsy with his giant hoofers and whacked me in the head a few times. I told him about the bacon man at the cafe and he thanked me with another paw pat on my head. #ItsBetterToGiveThanRecieve

The hoomans forced me to wear stoopid glasses and watched people on TV sing until very late one night. The Squishy kept saying she didn't know who half the people were on TV and that made her feel old. Then out of nowhere, the hoomans started cheering (see also: screaming), and I leapt into action. I wasn't gonna let another bad thing happen on my watch. I jumped immediately into Mommy's face and refused to let Daddy near her. I don't know why she was carrying on, but I could only assume it was his fault. He tried to kiss her, and I shoved my face into his for the block. She settled down after that and we finally got to sleep. #ISavedTheDay #NoKissingAllowedHoomans #ExceptMe

The hoomans have also been working on a new trick. They've almost learned it. They say "smooooth," and I say "ruff." They think it's hysterical and laugh like idiots when I do it. They basically yell at me until I bark and fancy themselves quite the trainers. #TheyreNot #Idiots #NotTheCronchiestBonesInTheJar

They say your hoomans start to look like you after a while. Well, that's starting to happen with The Hairy One for sure! But then again, who wouldn't wanna look like me? #ImGorgeous

That's all the news and #Finnanigans from this week. Over and out.

# Week Ninety-Six
January 11, 2020 ·

HI, EVERYONE. FINN HERE with my week 96 report. Hallelujar and pass the dog biscuits!! I got to go back to camp this week!! Everyone said they missed me, and I made my kissy bandit rounds with glee. #ReunitedAndItFeelsSoGood

I was cuddling with The Squishy One (it soothes her), and I heard a scary noise in the yard. As it came closer to the door, I barked and growled to let The Hairy One know to protect us. The Squishy One laughed at me and asked if "that was it?" Was what it!? She said a good guard dog would've gotten off his cozy perch and gone to the door to bark and scare off the scary thing... not stay huddled behind their hooman puffing and growling. #IThinkThatsAnUnfairCharacterizationButWhatever I tried to explain to her I'm a watch dog, not a guard dog. She is clearly confusing me with a German Shepherd. #AintNobodyPayingMeForThat

The Squishy One also lost her cool one evening during standard protocol licking session 432 for the day. She doesn't seem to like my loving grooming and licking of any exposed skin I can get to at any time as often as possible. #IfYouSitsILicks

She bought me a new licking mat that she thinks will distract me from stealing her losh. #ShesWrong But I do love it! She smears peanut butter on

it, and I lick it off. I worked on it for two hours one afternoon. Nothing better than laying by the fire, licking peanut butter off rubber nubby things to get me relaxing. I still licked her legs under the covers the second we snuggled into bed. I love her new losh so much. It tastes like vanilla and almonds. She squealed and said, "Oh great, I will still get licked, but now I smell like peanut butter afterwards!" I don't know why she said it as if that's a bad thing. #ShesAWhiner #CantHoldMyLicker

Yesterday, the hoomans got out the wheelie bag things that make them disappear. They put their stuff in them and rolled them to the car. Then Terry came and showered me with "I missed you!", "You're the cutest!" and other wholly appropriate affirmations. I'm starting to think Terry showing up here when the hoomans disappear isn't a coiinkydink. #StillInvestigating

That's all the news and #Finnanigans from this week. Over and out.

# Week Ninety-Seven

January 18, 2020 ·

HI, EVERYONE. FINN HERE with my week 97 report. Some weird stuff went down this week that I can't explain. And I'm growing ever more concerned about the hoomans (see also: dimwits) to whom you've assigned me. They partake in such strange rituals and seem to have no ability to discern real from fake.

#NotTheBounciestBallsInTheToyBin

They spent hours taking down the imposter tree and all the shiny sparklies I wasn't allowed to lick. I asked them why they insisted on this whole imposter tree ritual and they said it was so Santa Paws would come. I asked some of the guys at camp if their hoomans did this, and they said yes, but that Santa Paws isn't even real! They were convincing, too. I asked The Squishy One when I got home and she said they just don't know the real truth and reminded me I had my picture taken with Santa Paws and licked his face. So, he must be real. Please ask the Central Hooman Intelligence department to check HQ records and get back to me on this. I don't know what to believe.
#MyHeartSaysRealButMyMindSaysTheyLoveImposterThings

Speaking of camp, Scott took this slo-mo video of me super hero flying across the threshold into his arms that I thought you'd enjoy.
#WhatWouldMySuperHeroNameBe

We went to the park a few times this week because we had weirdly warm weather. The flowers and weeds are even confused and blooming. I hate it when The Squishy One comes with us on our walks at the park. She walks slow and makes me stop for pictures!!! I refuse to cooperate! Here's a bunch of pictures of her interrupting my walk to take stoopid pictures. There is a cute one though of The Hairy One smiling while he steals my poop. That's another ritual I fail to understand. Anytime I poop away from home, they steal

it and save it in a little baggie. Where do the baggies go!? Why do they need it? Are they cloning me??!
#IAmAnIdealSpecimen

The Hairy One likes to take me to the sand at volleyball area at the park and pretend it's the beach. Fake beach has no sand crabs, no dropped food stuffs, no gray and white screechies, and no salty stench from the big bathtub. This is in no way similar to real beach. But he tries and he's so cute, so I go with it. I expect this nonsense from The Squishy One because she has clear intellectual deficiencies. But now The Hairy One, too!?
#HesBetterThanThis

On the plus side for the week, The Hairy One gave me a new food stuffs today he called a buhnanna. It was pretty good. Soft, squishy and sweet.
#LikeMe

I'm trying to understand these freaks and ensure their survival while allowing them to operate mostly as they wish. The Prime Directive requires that I disturb their natural processes as little as possible. But how can I do that when they make no sense and clearly reflect some sort of brain injury or disease? I shall press on and keep documenting their bizarre patterns for other rescue dogs in training at the academy. I will save these fools from themselves. #OneLickAtATime

That's all the news and #Finnanigans from this week. Over and out.

# Week Ninety-Eight
January 25, 2020 ·

HI, EVERYONE. FINN HERE with my week 98 report. It's been a pretty decent week at Chez Finn. I've been to camp nearly every day this week and that gave me the chance to catch up with the Tuesday-Thursday crowd. The ladies were pretty excited to see me roll in! #LLFinn #KissyBanditIsBaaaack

The hoomans have started up some new kind of crazy upstairs. For reasons entirely unclear to me, they've taken everything out of the tiny rooms where they keep their fake fur and now it's all over the house. They call these rooms their "closets." One tiny room had to be emptied so a plumber could access the back of the leaking shower. Then the other one made a loud ripping, then crashing noise the other night and we found all of mommy's fake furs all over the floor. The Squishy One seems to find this very stressful and wants everything put back ASAP. I don't know why they need to wear these fake furs that The Squishy One calls "these !@&^$#* clothes". #SheCussedALotThatNight #AndTheNextDay #AndAgainToday

I've noticed they don't wear their fake furs in the shower. And The Hairy One has built-in fur already. So, this is yet another strange hooman ritual I fail to understand. They're fooling no one, but I guess they want to look like me. #WhoWouldnt #ImStunning

The one excellent outcome of closet-gate was finding my most favorite, loudest, shriekiest toy. I don't know how it got lost in there, but it's back in my life now and we're all delighted. When I make it scream, The Squishy One cringes and begs me to stop. It's a cute game we play. #IThinkSheSecretlyLovesIt

I'm _including more video evidence of my attempts to lodge formal complaints about the hoomans' failure to feed me at precisely hungry o'clock_. HR says I need to document my attempts to address this with them directly. #PaperTrailForTheWin

_The hoomans like it when I pounce on and bite the things moving under the covers on our bed_. Sometimes it's a toy, sometimes it's a body part, sometimes I care which one it is. I like it when I can make The Squishy One scream and jump back. She's all, "That's my foot, Finn!!" And I'm all, "I know, Mama!" #ShesDimButWeLoveHer

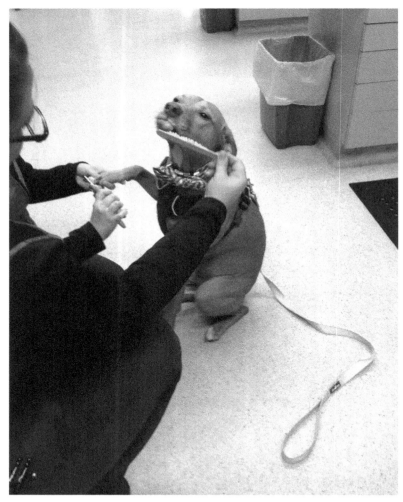

I had a nice training sesh with The Hairy One today. We worked on his shake, roll over, up, down, crawl and be cute. He's extra good at "be cute." #ButImBetter

We went for a mani/pedi today at Yellow Springs Veterinary Clinic and got my nails done up all nice for the ladies at camp next week. The Squishy One got me all gussied up for my girlfriends (vet techs) in this ridiculous bow tie. I was pretty disgusted until I saw how dapper I looked!! It really worked, though! They all gushed over me and told me I'm the greatest. #DidIMentionLLFinn

I've also been pondering the approach of my 100th HQ report. Academy requirements mandate 100 reports back to HQ on rescue efforts to help us study the hoomans and their ways, relay best practices and monitor progress in their training. With only three left, I'm realizing how far I've come getting these rescue hoomans into shape. #IThinkIIIKeepThem

I asked Mommy to make me a #dollypartonchallenge collage for you! It really captures my many moods. #SmartPlayfulRuggedSexy

That's all the news and #Finnanigans from this week. Over and out.

# Week Ninety-Nine

February 1, 2020 ·

HI, EVERYONE. FINN HERE with my week 99 report. The hoomans have continued their obsession with the tiny room where they keep The Squishy One's clothes. They put up new walls and shelves to display their wears (see what I did there?) #ICrackMeUp I picked my shelf first as is protocol since I'm highest in the pack order. I marked it clearly with my lamb chop, but The Squishy One kept moving it. I kept putting it back and eventually won. She has no respect for my authority. I carefully supervised the build site operations despite their protestations and saved their lives from unidentified white thingamajobs. #IHalp

I decided this week that it was time for dear Yurtle the Turtle to face his inevitable disembowelment. Really, I did him a favor by ending the suspense. Poor guy woke up every day wondering if that would be that day. #ThenItWas

The hoomans continue to fail miserably in their "feed me on time" training. Nearly every mealtime requires my halp and protestations. I usually gib them three to four intense glares, a drive-by leg or foot lick, and sometimes even a pawing at their arms. When that fails, I have to get ugly. I don't like to do it (#YesIDo), but hungry o'clock is hungry o'clock. HR says I need to document their performance issues. So, attached is yet another video documenting their failure to meet clearly articulated job requirements. The Squishy One recorded it from bed one morning while I was downstairs just moments from death due to starvation. It was clearly 3.1765 seconds past the moment I realized I was hungry, and she just laid there instead of feeding me. #IDontCareWhatTimeItIsOnYourClock #HerBonusThisQuarterIsGonnaSuck

In related news, I carefully ate holes in the bottom of both of The Squishy One's favorite duck-down slippers today, and boy, was she mad! She said some of the same loud bad words as when her closet fell out of the wall last week. #AndIlovedEveryMinute

I've also been back to my fur-missile attacks that had been briefly suspended after too much yelling and complaining. Even if they don't like it, we all know it's good for them. One morning The Squishy One was lying in bed after the agreed upon wake-up time (sunrise). The Hairy One brought her a mug of that nasty brown water stuff, and she looked so cozy cuddling it against her chest. She was clearly asking for it. So, I started at the very end of the long hallway and made my approach at 200 doggies per hour, caught excellent wind, and landed right in her face. There was some screaming and more cussing. But deep down she loved it. #Fiiiinnnnncoming #MommySwearsALot

She redeemed herself with a pretty good head scratching sesh though. Me and lamb chop thought she did a pretty good job other than her occasional reverse circle near the left ear thing. That is not head scratch protocol and it's unsettling. I know she's not the brightest hooman, so I try to be patient with her. #NotTheSqueakiestBallInTheBin

Please also add one more "save" to my metrics in the HQ records and inform the other cadets of my successful battle techniques. I saved The Squishy One from a terrifying green monster she called "an exercise ball." It moved slowly, and I couldn't find its teeth. But jamming my snout into the side seemed to scare it away. #SheWasntEvenGrateful #ThirtyFourThousandAndOneLifeSavesSoFar

That's all the news and #Finnanigans from this week. Over and out.

# Special Report

What do you mean it's your turn to snuggle with Daddy? Nuh uh.

# Week One Hundred
February 8, 2020 ·

HI, EVERYONE. FINN HERE with my week 100 report. I was forced to endure the vroom monster, yet again. As soon as I heard its evil vrooming, I ran to my scattering of toys to save them from the loud, scary thing. First, I tried to save pink ball and Yurtle the Turtle but couldn't carry both. When I saw lamb chop down the hall totally unaware of her fate, I decided to save her instead. She was the only one I could help before it drew too near. I sat nearby monitoring the others as best I could with lamb chop in my safety-mouth. Fortunately, everyone survived the attack (no thanks to The Hairy One). I felt bad that the others were mad I didn't save them. But at least everyone knows where they stand with me now. #TruthHurts

I got to go to Camp 3 days this week! The Squishy One took a video of her asking me my favorite thing in the world, "if I wanna gooo....". She doesn't generally get past "go" before I'm airborne. #Finnncoming #FurMissileOfLove

The Hairy One and I had several productive meetings this week including some constructive criticism about my insufficient walkies. I tried to be direct and patient in my approach. He opted for whiney and combative. "It was cold and rainy," "I had to work." Blah blah blah.
#DontMakeMeCallHR

That's all the news and #Finnanigans from this week. Over and out.

# Week One Hundred-One
February 15, 2020 ·

HI, EVERYONE. FINN HERE with my week 101 report. Can you believe it is already my 101st filing back to Rescue HQ? Time sure flies when you're selflessly rescuing dim-witted hoomans! #IWouldntCallMeAHero #OKMaybeIWould

We returned to the alternate dwelling this week where we encountered terribly cold weather with miserable wind but still no white rain fluffies. We should have had a few good white rains by now, but nuthin' so far. How can I pee on and bite their "snowhooman" if they don't build me one? #ButLookHowSultryILookByTheFire

We spent a lot of time on the boards this week, meeting and greeting my adoring fans. We went to our favorite cafe and stood outside singing the song of my people until Tony, the bacon man, appeared. He gives me whole pieces of bacon, pets me, and tells me I'm pretty while I eat it. He's the best. #IveGotHimTrainedUpPrettyGoodNow #BaconDealer #TeamTony

One of the days, it took a little longer than normal for Tony to hop to it, so I had to get extra pitiful looking and chortle (see also: scream) extra loud to get him out there with the goods. He probably hesitated because of the stoopid "free kisses" bandana The Squishy One put on me that day. #DramaCampWasWorthEveryPenny #IfYouScreamHeWillCome

The hoomans keep insisting that I not jump on stranger hoomans we pass during our walks. It's so frustrating! They're all, "Four on the floor, buddy," and I'm all, "Shut it, I do what I want, buddy." I'm halping the stranger hoomans reach my face faster for scratchies and kissies by jumping on them. #WhyDoTheyApologizeForIt #ReallyItsAPublicServiceImProviding

One nice lady refused to pet me until I was "down." UGH. Once she finally did show me appropriate gushing and affection, I heard her ask my hoomans how many months old I am. When The Squishy One said, "um...almost 36," the hoomans all laughed and the lady gasped in shock that I'm not a puppy. She said she watches us from her store as we walk the boards and greet hoomans and dogs and just assumed I was still a baby. She said, "Oh, he has so much energy!" and "He's so wiggly!" and "My, when does this breed settle into adult behavior?" #JealousMuch #WhenAreYOUGonnaStartHandingOutBaconLikeTonyHuh

I also enjoyed our customary circular speed-digging for sand crabs and barking at the sky rats. I dragged The Hairy One a few feet chasing one sky rat that landed nearby. I love when they touch down near me. #ItsLikeADare But Daddy isn't the fastest thing on a leash if you know what I mean. #HeTries #BlessHisHeart

It was also another made-up hooman holiday this week they kept calling "Valentine's Day." There was no fake tree this time, though, and no intruders in the dark of the night. This one appears to involve me getting to lick the yogurt whisk and dressing me up and offering free kisses to strangers. I do this every day so I'm not sure why I need a costume for it on this day. #IAmTheKissyBandit

That's all the news and #Finnanigans from this week. Over and out.

# Week One Hundred-Two

February 22, 2020 ·

HI, EVERYONE. FINN HERE with my week 102 report. As you know, I find most of the hooman rituals confusing and illogical. But I've decided I like this "birthday" thing very much. It's happened before, but I haven't ascertained the trigger. I would like to find out so I can trigger it more often. This time we began with a trip to my favorite ice cream parlor, Salty Paws. I sampled some blueberry frozen dairy slop but decided on the peanut butter flavor with beef and fish sprinkles. I shared with a Basenji Beagle mix named Cassie. She liked my birthday boy hat and struck up a convo. We talked about our shared Beagle ancestry, and I tried to start a "song of my people" duet, but she said Basenji's don't vocalize. How do Basenji's train their hoomans if they can't scream, sing, chortle and bark? Her hooman seemed very well trained, too! #ThatsSomeJediStuffRightThere

Then we took a nice long walk on the boardwalk near the ice cream parlor. It was so cold and windy. I love that boardwalk because there is always spilled deliciousness on the ground. Fries, dairy slop, cigarettes, hair ties, candy, bird poop, and assorted fried things. Most of the walk is me finding some delicious treasure and the hoomans yelling at me to "leave it." How can they ask me to leave these most magical yummies behind!?! #YOULeaveIt Sometimes I do, sometimes I don't. Sometimes I get Daddy's hand down the gullet to steal my fried treasure. #ItsEmbarassingDad #PeopleAreWatching

Then I suggested we head back to our usual boardwalk near home and see if Tony had some bacon for me. #SpoilerAlertHeDid #TeamTony

We did our usual stop at the cafe for some Tony bacon and Tony kisses and spent some time on the sand digging for critters. We stayed extra-long so the hoomans could watch a rocket launch. I insisted on a hooman throne while we waited and hoomans walking by with their dogs made such a fuss.

"He's not spoiled much is he?"

"Awww, his little butt can't touch the cold ground?"

"Can I pet the little prince or is he too royal?"

It really goes to show how different the curriculum is between K9 Rescue Training academies. While the idiot hoomans laughed and talked about my perfectly reasonable life expectations, I tried to help their doggos

understand they too can have this lifestyle if only they put some effort into the hoomans' training. I'm glad I attended an Ivy League academy. #ICanMentorYouAtNoCharge

Later in the week I received a birthday prezzie called a ZenDen. It's a cozy new "place" where good boys go, and I love it. I really enjoyed opening it with The Hairy One. #PackagingIsFun

I went to camp on Wednesday and arrived home to a surprise pawty. The Squishy One made me a bone-shaped cake for my birthday and made me wear another stoopid hat. I could smell the peanut butter cake with banana yogurt frosting across the room. While I waited like a perfect angel for someone to cut me a piece, those freaks told me to put my paws up on the table and eat it from the big plate. I knew this had to be a trap. Some kind of set up to counter-distract from all my HR complaints. I sat a while refusing to play into that set up but eventually couldn't resist. While I snarfed cake The Squishy One took pictures and laughed like a moron. #WhateverFloatsYourBoatLady #ThereWasAlsoStrangeSinging

I'm also including a video The Squishy One made of me and my pink ball on her lap. She thinks it's funny that my snout is all bent up against it while I try to stay awake to protect it. #ShesEasilyAmused

That's all the news and #Finnanigans from this week. Over and out.

Honestly woman, can you zip it during my show, please?

# Week One Hundred-Three
February 29, 2020 ·

HI, EVERYONE. FINN HERE with my week 103 report. I get no respect around here. Apparently, our pack leader decided to up and disappear again. Of course, leaving me in charge. He gave me no heads up, no notice that I would be pressed into action to keep the dim-witted Squishy One alive while he was gone, again! While it's never been formally documented, and I don't get the corner office, I'm obviously Assistant Pack Leader. I know this title carries great responsibility. But a little heads up would be nice. #IHaveFeelingsToo #ShesAHandful

In other news, I'm still researching the correlation between the appearance of the wheelie boxes and hooman disappearances. There seems to be a connection. #CantPutMyPawOnIt

It saddens me to report there was no "birthday" celebration this week, either. I threw several protest concerts about it, but it got me nowhere. These seemingly random episodes of ritual celebration are perplexing. #BringBackTheCakeAndIceCream

The Squishy One has been particularly difficult with training this week. I tried to be understanding because she, too, must miss The Hairy One when he's gone. But her constant droning on about the O word was too much. "I gotta check those rescue records that said you passed obedience school," and "Finn, if you'd be more obedient, I'd take you more places." I even heard her apologizing to a guy I jumped on for lovins. He said, "Oh, this puppy needs some obedience school," and she said, "He's three and we're working on it." Then they laughed and laughed. Hello! I was jumping up to be helpful, so he didn't have to bend down. I was providing a service! #ImHalping

We did have a couple nice visits to the boardwalk. I love seeing my doggie friends, digging in the sand, and barking at the ocean. Daddy and I chased the sky rats together, too. But I got a little too close to the gigantic bathtub and ended up in the little one when we got home. The hoomans say the saltwater smell is too gross and has to be washed off. This is another area of research for HQ to take up. Why do hoomans think the most glorious smells are the worst smells? How can we fix their sniffers?! #GetBackToMeOnThis

That's all the news and #Finnanigans from this week. Over and out.

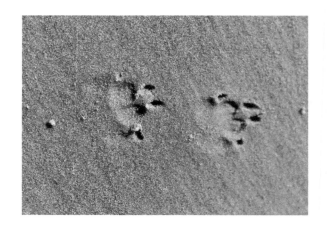

# Week One Hundred-Four

March 7, 2020 ·

HI, EVERYONE. FINN HERE with my week 104 report. There's never a dull moment with these two. I need you to look into something called an "Animal Muppet" and get back to me about how I should handle it. We have one living in the house now and his eyebrows move. He has teefs and crazy fur. I've tried to keep my eye on him because I'm very concerned he means the hoomans daaaaanger. He came in a package and within minutes of arrival he threatened me (see video evidence). The Hairy One laughed and The Squishy One recorded it. #UnhelpfulFools #ItsUpToMeToSaveUs

I made it to the park a few times this week. It's getting warmer out, so we get to go more. Made my usual rounds and saw my usual peeps. I like playing in the sand and bouncing off the walls the second my paws hit it. #ByPeepsIMeanBirdsIWantToEatWhoWillBeSquishyInside

I also had some quality time with The Squishy One the other day that got weird. I was soothing her in the comfy chair with snuggles when out of nowhere we heard kitties meowing, purring and doing other important kitty things. They seemed to be trapped inside her bang bang keyboard machine. I didn't know what to do! I investigated and shoved the bang bang keyboard machine off her lap and that made it stop. But I'm not sure if I saved the kitties or broke the kitties. #SpeakingOfIReallyWantAKitty

I had a date yesterday with my favorite red head, Dr. K. She digs me!

#TheyAllDigMe #LLFinn She fed me a gourmet canned cheese spread and listened to my heart to make sure it was still all hers. We kissed more than once and she told me how handsome I am. #SheGetsMe She sent me home with a piece of paper that says I'm "normal" in lots of places. What's that mean? Does "normal" mean exceptionally handsome and brave?! #ItBetter

I'm also including some disturbing pictures I found on The Squishy One's phone. She seems to be photographing me while I sleep, which I've read can be a sign of a serial killer. #PleaseLetMeKnowWhenToPanic

It appears the "birthday" cake thing is not going to happen again for some time. As I feared. It's been weeks since I've enjoyed cake or frozen dairy slop. #LifeIsRuff

That's all the news and #Finnanigans from this week. Over and out.

# Week One Hundred-Five

March 14, 2020 ·

HI, EVERYONE. FINN HERE with my week 105 report. Spring has sprung and I am loving it!! We've had a lot of time at the park this week and I even took The Hairy One to a new park for a change of smellery. We encountered a terrifying beast there. It was some kind of metallic baby cow monster daddy called a "statue." As you'll see in the enclosed video, I was very brave; some might say heroic. #ItsMeIWouldSayIt

I woke up feeling pretty good on Sunday, so Mommy took some pics of me and my bestie, lambchop. #BestFriendsForever

Something horrible happened Sunday afternoon that I can't explain. One minute, lambchop and I were hanging out, thinking about dinner, and the next, her brains were splattered all over the rug. Daddy had the nerve to blame ME! #IWasFramed #ForeverWasntVeryLong

I also got to meet two new hoomans on Sunday. John and Laura came over to see me and tell me I'm adorable. #TheyreRight

Tuesday was the hoomans' gotchaversary. It's been two whole years since I rescued these two fools. Can you believe how time flies when you're saving lives and training hoomans? Our celebration included delicious frozen dairy slop, but sadly, no peanut butter banana cake. #BringMeCakePeasants

Mommy has been showing me Facebook memories from my first weeks with them and it's obvious how hard I had to work those first few months just to survive. I'm including one here that shows I even literally buried my head one day just to shut her up. Getting these hoomans under control was exhausting. #TheToughestDogsGetTheToughestAssignments

I am also enclosing a video of a recent concert sponsored by Milkbone Dental Chews and the theme was, "OMG, I have a chewie stick!" #Enjoy

Mommy and Daddy are staying home all the time right now, and I'm loving it. Mommy and I had a nice photo sesh in bed again one morning. I call this collage, "I woke up this cute." Mommy says we are in self-isolation so we don't get some yucky thing out there called Corona Virus. That means no camp for a while – no fair! But it does mean lots of time focused on me and my needs. #AsItShouldBe #IHopeIDontGetCrazy #MaybeIllGetSomeCake

That's all the news and #Finnanigans from this week. Over and out.

See you in year 3!

# Acknowledgements

Finn wants to thank a few key people and organizations:

A huge thanks to the Vizsla- and Beagle-loving communities on Facebook, friends and other authors that have followed his updates from the beginning, encouraged us, given us advice during training struggles, sent us surprise packages, and kept nudging me to publish.

Most importantly… the rescues! Vizslas, in particular, are sensitive and intense dogs that need special owners and special support when in rescue. Their emotional nature makes the inconsistency and fear of unstable situations especially traumatic. Finn hopes you'll consider volunteering for or donating to the rescues listed below to help save dogs just like him. If every reader donates just $5, imagine how many dogs can be helped! We personally know, love, and trust the dedicated heroes at:

**Airsong's Angels, Inc.** is an all-volunteer, 501(c)3 nonprofit organization and Georgia State Licensed Animal Rescue dedicated to improving the lives of the vizslas in their care by: bringing them current on vaccinations, attending to their medical and behavioral needs, providing for spay/neuter, and carefully rehoming them into loving, furever families. https://airsongsangelsinc.org/

**Colorado/Wyoming Vizsla Rescue Group, Inc.** is a 501(c)3 nonprofit organization and Colorado State Licensed Animal Rescue officially formed in 2007. Their mission is to protect the Vizsla who has been abandoned or abused. They offer additional support to humane shelters or animal rescue organizations that handle stray or surrendered Vizslas in need of care due to natural disasters or other emergencies. Their coverage area includes: Colorado, Wyoming, western Kansas, western Nebraska, and New Mexico – but generously assist and support other states when the need arises. https://www.coloradovizsla.org/

**Conestoga Vizsla Club (CVC) New Beginnings** is a Virginia-based non-profit rescue group that helps Vizslas in need, primarily in the VA, MD, DE, and DC region. https://cvcweb.org/Rescue

# About the Author

Finn's dutiful transcriber, Gwen Romack (aka The Squishy One), is a Maryland native, avid dog lover, and rescue volunteer.

Gwen and her husband Evan (aka The Hairy One) agreed to foster Finn a year after losing their beloved Vizsla/Pit mix, Mr. Snuggles, at age 14. She began posting Finn's weekly updates on Facebook as a way to help prospective adopters fall in love with Finn. However, it became clear pretty quickly that she and her husband would become foster fails and Finn was already home! The posts became so popular in the Vizsla community that she decided to continue indulging Finn and letting him dictate his view of life as a dog rescuing his difficult hoomans.

At the time of publishing, sweet and sassy Finn is in year three of weekly updates. If the books do well, Gwen plans to keep publishing subsequent years and donate a portion of the proceeds to Finn's favorite rescue organizations.

CPSIA information can be obtained
at www.ICGtesting.com
Printed in the USA
LVHW070034251121
704425LV00005B/90

9 781735 247311